KLINCK MEMORIAL LIBRARY
Concordia College
River Forest, IL 60305

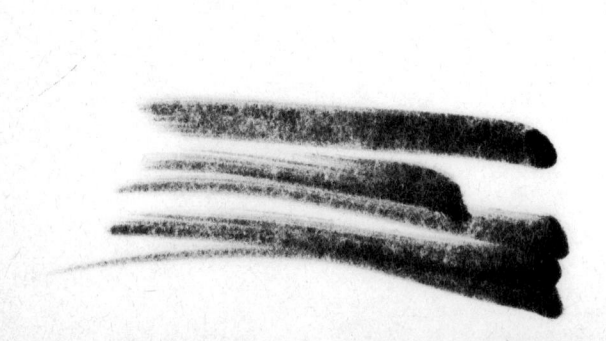

the MEDIEVAL FRENCH MONARCHY

the MEDIEVAL FRENCH MONARCHY

John Bell Henneman
University of Iowa

KLINCK MEMORIAL LIBRARY
Concordia College
River Forest, IL   60305

The Dryden Press
901 North Elm Street
Hinsdale, Illinois 60521

Copyright © 1973 by The Dryden Press
All Rights Reserved
Library of Congress Catalog Card Number: 72-14006
ISBN: 03-086630-8
Printed in the United States of America
 345 090 98765432

Cover Credit
Detail of St. Louis (Louis IX) from the
Psalter of St. Louis.
The Piermont Morgan Library

Contents

	Introduction	1
Part One	**Disintegration of the Carolingian Monarchy**	13
1 *Jan Dhondt*	Nationalism and the Territorial Principalities	15
2 *Archibald R. Lewis*	The Failure of Public Authority in Languedoc	20
Part Two	**Change of Dynasty in 987**	27
3 *Jean François Lemarignier*	The Contracting Sphere of Royal Influence	29
4 *Joseph Calmette*	A Feudal Lord on the Throne	35

Part Three		**Revival of Kingship under the Capetians**	39
5	*Marc Bloch*	The Capetian Miracle of Healing	41
6	*Jean François Lemarignier*	Signs of Revival after 1077	45
7	*Achille Luchaire*	Louis VI and the Enforcement of Justice	52
8	*Marcel Pacaut*	From Grandeur to Prudence: The Policy of Louis VII	57
9	*Robert Fawtier*	The Great Kings of the Dynasty	64
10	*Jean de Joinville*	Louis IX, the Embodiment of Morality and Justice	71
11	*James W. Fesler*	The Emergence of Provincial Administration	76
12	*Jan Rogozinski*	The Lawyers of Languedoc in Local Government	83
13	*Franklin J. Pegues*	The Role of Lawyers in the Central Government	89
Part Four		**The Enigma of Philip the Fair**	93
14	*Joseph R. Strayer*	Philip IV: A King Who Was Constitutional	95
15	*Bryce Lyon*	Philip IV: A King Who Avoided Being Constitutional	102
Part Five		**Developing Institutions of Government**	109
16	*Elizabeth A. R. Brown*	Philip IV and the Morality of Taxation	111
Part Six		**Insecurity, Crisis, and Triumph: The 14th and 15th Centuries**	121
17	*Raymond Cazelles*	Politics and Factions under Philip VI	123
18	*Edouard Perroy*	The Panic and Defeat of John II	130
19	*Peter S. Lewis*	The Valois Kings and Their Final Triumph	136
		Suggestions for Further Reading	144

the MEDIEVAL FRENCH MONARCHY

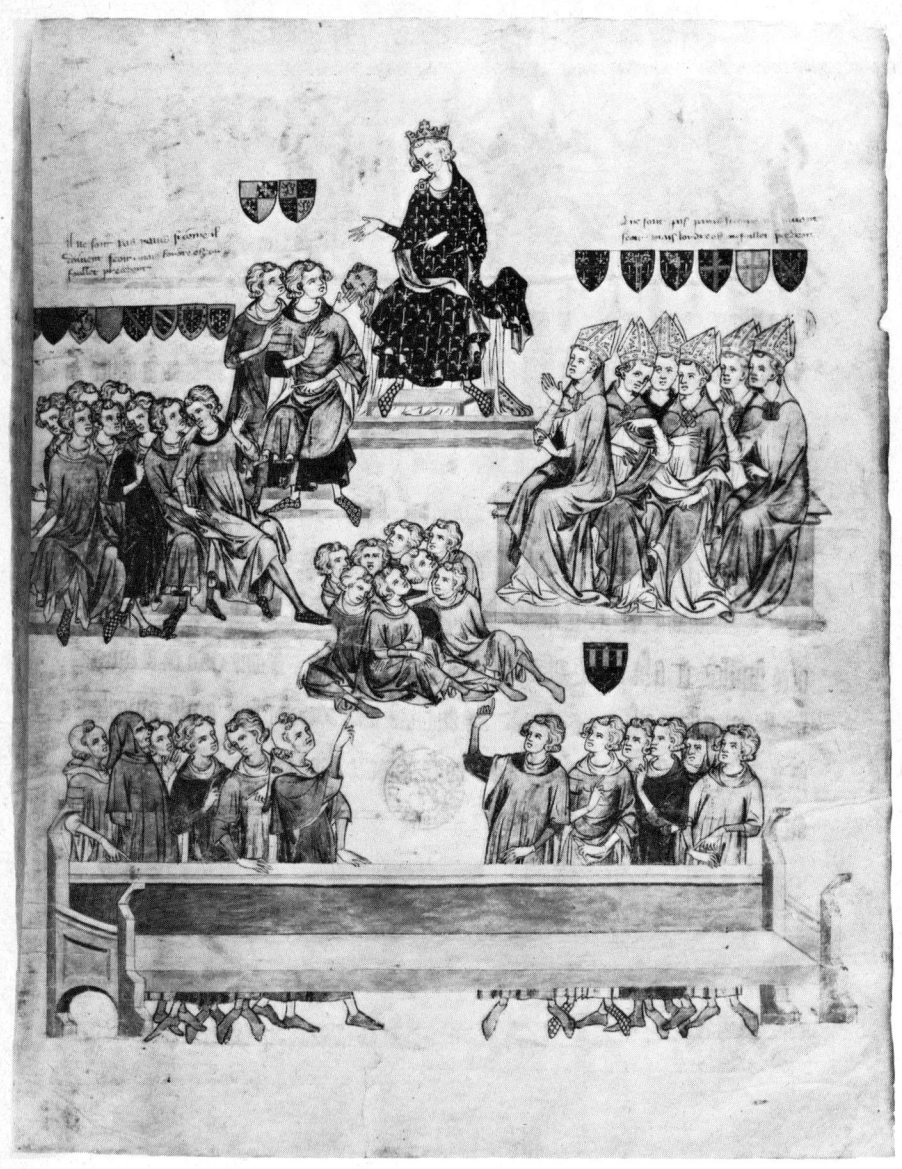

Philip VI of France with Council, 1332. Miniature from *Actes du Proces de Robert d'Artois*.
Credit: Bibliotheque Nationale, Paris.

Introduction

The French monarchy is often cited to illustrate the main lines of European political development in the Middle Ages and Renaissance. The empire of Charlemagne disintegrated in the ninth century, and for three hundred years government was largely in the hands of feudal lords. Gradual revival of royal authority under the twelfth-century kings of the Capetian family culminated in the triumphs of Philip II (r. 1180-1223). Thereafter, feudal monarchy gradually gave way to a stronger, more bureaucratic regime. This trend, interrupted by a period of weakness during the Hundred Years' War (1337-1453), eventually led to the establishment of a strong national state in the late fifteenth and sixteenth centuries.

This brief sketch may be adequate as an outline of French political development, but many of the crucial steps have long been matters of scholarly debate. Important research in the years since 1940 has resolved some of the problems while bringing others into sharper focus. Historians now have a much clearer picture of emerging feudalism, the timing and nature of the Capetian revival, the growth of the royal bureaucracy, the obstacles confronting the establishment of permanent taxation, and the crisis of the monarchy in the fourteenth century.

Most of the selections included in this book have been published since World War II, a majority of them in the 1960s. They document the most important steps in the evolution of monarchy in medieval France and bear upon the problems most interesting to contemporary scholars; yet many of their conclusions have not yet found their way into general textbooks. These writings are intended to introduce students to the major problems and current historiography in this field.

The Franks, a Germanic people living in the Netherlands, conquered the Roman province of Gaul under their first great king, Clovis I (r. 481-511), whose successors are known as the Merovingians. Clovis was baptized as a Roman Catholic by St. Rémy, and the subsequent Frankish conquests had considerable backing from the Church. Although the Merovingians conquered a large part of Europe north of the Alps, the area of heavy Frankish settlement *(Francia)* was between the Loire and Rhine rivers. The western part of this territory (Neustria, or France Minor) became fairly Romanized, while the eastern part (Austrasia) remained largely Germanic. The seventh century Merovingians lost power to the landed aristocracy, especially the wealthy Pippinid family of Austrasia, which began to monopolize the leading position in the royal household, that of *major domus,* or "mayor of the palace." This family became known as the Carolingians, after Charles Martel (mayor, 714-741), whose military victories laid the groundwork for the brilliant but short-lived Frankish empire of his successors.

Acting with the cooperation of the Church, Charles' son Pepin deposed the last Merovingian in 751 and was anointed king of the Franks in a religious ceremony. Pepin's son, Charles the Great (Charlemagne, r. 768-814), conquered the northern parts of Italy and Spain as well as the remaining Germanic tribes in central Europe. The ruler of virtually all of Latin Christendom, except the British Isles, Charlemagne was crowned emperor by Pope Leo III in 800.

The Carolingian conquests of the eighth century were accomplished by an army based increasingly on heavy cavalry. Cavalry service was expensive, and the money in circulation was very limited. To build up the army, the Carolingians had to supply their followers with landed estates, which were worked by peasants and would yield enough income to support a mounted warrior. Beginning with Charles Martel they used Church lands and conquered territory for this purpose, but Charlemagne's successors weakened the monarchy by alienating the royal estates. Military service, long the honorable obligation of all free men, became synonymous with cavalry service and was limited to wealthy landlords who became a military elite supported by the vast peasant population, which was too poor to afford mounted service.

The economic and political institutions of the early ninth century were incapable of sustaining a large territorial state, and Charlemagne's empire depended largely on the emperor's personality and the close cooperation of the Church. Local government was in the hands of counts, most of them Frankish aristocrats, whose power was checked by roving inspectors called *missi dominici*. Charlemagne tried to reinforce this rudimentary regime by installing trusted followers, called *vassi dominici,* in each *pagus* (county) and by having the counts and greater magnates swear oaths of loyalty and become his *fideles.*

Under Charlemagne's son Louis the Pious and his successors, the empire quickly disintegrated. Seaborne raiders, like the North African Moslems ("Saracens") and the dreaded Vikings from Scandinavia, pillaged the river valleys with impunity. Furthermore, the division of the empire among Charlemagne's grandsons led to bitter family quarrels. And the great landowners (the principal military class) were able to sell their vassalage to the highest bidder, receiving benefices of lands, which they soon were able to turn into hereditary fiefs over which the kings had little, if any, practical control.

The medieval French monarchy first appeared as a separate political entity when the Carolingian empire was divided according to treaties in 843 and 870. The West Frankish kingdom created at this time was a good deal smaller than modern France, with the Rhone and Saône rivers marking its eastern border. In the 880s the empire was briefly reunited under Charles the Fat, of the German branch of the Carolingian family. He proved totally inept in the face of the Viking threat and was deposed in 887. For their new king, the West Franks turned to a member of the aristocracy, Eudes, of the Robertian family, who had been count of Paris. The need to organize effective defenses at the local level encouraged the spread of vassalage and increased the prestige of local strongmen like Eudes who were able to defend their regions better than the more distant king.

The two selections in Part I are concerned with the events that followed the disintegration of the Carolingian monarchy. In much of the West Frankish kingdom, the accession of Eudes was not recognized, and other local rulers became virtually independent of the crown. Jan Dhondt believes that the kingdom then broke into a dozen or more territorial principalities whose development was favored by the resentment of subject nationalities against Frankish rule. In a recent study by Archibald Lewis, however, Dhondt's thesis has been challenged. Confining his research to the most southern parts of the kingdom (Languedoc and Catalonia), Lewis found little evidence of nationalism. He concludes that public power in the south disintegrated so rapidly as to frustrate the establishment of territorial states.

In the face of growing separatism but a rapidly receding Viking threat, the West Frankish throne passed back and forth between the Carolingian and Robertian families, until Louis IV was recalled from exile in 936 and a definitive Carolingian restoration was attempted. This effort did not produce a stronger monarchy, but the Carolingians retained the throne until the sudden death of Louis V in 987. The magnates then rejected Charles of Lorraine, the Carolingian heir, and turned again to the Robertian family, bestowing the crown on Hugh Capet.

The reigns of Hugh and his first successors, now known as the Capetians, have been a subject of disagreement among historians. In Part II, two different views are presented about the change of dynasty in 987. Jean-François Lemarignier has studied the diplomas and charters issued by these kings. He has found that the recipients of such documents, and the personnel who undersigned or witnessed them, changed significantly in the eleventh century, with important implications for royal power. Regarding the change of dynasty in 987, Lemarignier acknowledges the traditional view that the events of that year had little real significance, but he argues that a sharp new decline in royal authority occurred soon after. No longer able to rule in the Carolingian fashion with the counsel of their *fideles* (the greater prelates and territorial princes), the kings were surrounded by persons of increasingly lower social rank, and their charters were applied to an increasingly restricted geographical area.

Is it then correct to view the accession of Hugh Capet as the signal for a new decline, or would it be more accurate to say, with Joseph Calmette, that the monarchy merely acquired a new orientation? Calmette found the election of Hugh significant because it brought to the throne a feudal lord, who called himself both duke and king, a man whose attitudes were those of a seigneur and territorial prince. Such a man could comfortably abandon imperial ambitions and rule his own principality in the Ile-de-France without being diverted by projects beyond his capabilities. The Capetians did not scorn the royal title, of course, and Calmette credits Hugh with considerable shrewdness in having his son Robert crowned as king-designate. This action, repeated in later generations, perpetuated the Capetian hold on the throne.

The six selections in Part III deal with the revival of kingship under the Capetians. The earliest manifestation of this revival may have been the remarkable legend of royal healing powers, which Marc Bloch has studied. From the time of Pepin in the eighth century, the king had been anointed in a sacred ceremony and had acquired a quasi-priestly character that set him apart from ordinary princes. Beginning with Hugh's son, Robert II (r. 996-1031), it was believed that the king's touch could cure scrofula, and Bloch has suggested that this miraculous attribute strengthened the mystique of Capetian kingship. The monarchy could also claim other advantages—a tradition of close ties with the Church, the ancient concept of the king as dispenser of justice, and some theoretical basis for asserting suzerainty over the territorial princes.

By themselves, these factors could not guarantee a revival of royal authority, and Lemarignier argues, in a second selection, that the crown's fortunes reached their lowest ebb in the half century that ended in 1077. After this date, he finds the first clear indications of reviving authority, coinciding with the so-called Gregorian reform of the Church. This movement was marked by the spread of large federations of reformed monasteries under the leadership of great religious sanctuaries such as Cluny in Burgundy. A new spirit of hierarchy and order made itself felt, and this spirit began to penetrate the king's circle. Lemarignier has suggested two early signs of the coming royal recovery: the rising influence of the great officers of the crown, and the appearance of a new and more authoritative kind of royal document, the writ, or *mandement*.

Signs of the monarchy's revival became pronounced in the reign of Louis VI (r. 1108-1137). Achille Luchaire argued that the key to this monarch's success was his long and relentless struggle to enforce royal justice in the Ile-de-France. Louis VI succeeded in imposing punishments on those renegade barons who despoiled the Church and crown. At his death in 1137, he left the monarchy with enhanced prestige and a royal domain in which the king's justice was enforced and respected.

Despite a brilliant marriage to Eleanor of Aquitaine, heiress to vast territories in southwestern France, Louis VII (r. 1137-1180) has traditionally been regarded as a weaker monarch than his father. The first years of his reign were marked by grand but unsuccessful projects and the failure of his marriage. Yet even his unfortunate crusade yielded some advantages, for it made him an international figure and led to the first royal presence in Languedoc in many generations. Marcel Pacaut argues that Louis VII was more effective than was once believed, thanks to a change in his policies in the 1150s. Thereafter he devoted his efforts to cooperating with the Church and to building up the royal domain on which his real power depended. Rather than seeing Louis VII as weak and indecisive, Pacaut credits the king and his new advisers with conscious policies that strengthened the monarchy for its coming struggle with the kings of England.

Geoffrey Plantagenet, count of Anjou (r. 1129-1151), had married the daughter of Henry I of England and then conquered Normandy. His son Henry inherited Normandy and Anjou, then married Eleanor of Aquitaine after her divorce from Louis. In 1154 he became king of England as Henry II and thus put together an Anglo-French empire, the continental part of which alone dwarfed the holdings of Louis VII. For the rest of the Middle Ages the Plantagenets were to be the great enemies of the French kings. Louis VII maintained himself by exploiting quarrels in the Plantagenet family and his own superior feudal position. It was left to the next French king, Philip II, to reverse the balance of power.

The best known kings of the Capetian dynasty are Philip II, called Philip Augustus, and his grandson Louis IX, known as St. Louis. Is it correct to treat them as greater than their twelfth century predecessors, or did they merely profit from the work of these ancestors? Robert Fawtier has suggested that Philip II (r. 1180-1223) was blessed by good fortune as well as skill. He was an able politician who carefully exploited his legal position as feudal overlord. First adding some important northern territories to the royal domain, he achieved his great triumph shortly after 1200. He seized the rich lands of Normandy and Anjou from John of England when the latter failed to answer a summons to Philip's court. Philip and his successors also profited from the religious war known as the Albigensian crusade, as it enabled them to acquire most of Languedoc for the royal domain.

It is more difficult to assess the greatness of Louis IX (r. 1226-1270). A beloved figure, widely regarded as a saint in his own lifetime, Louis reigned for four decades over a kingdom that assumed the cultural and political leadership of Europe. Yet his predecessors had prepared the way for this hegemony, and Fawtier credits the king's mother, Blanche of Castile, with great skill in defeating the feudal rebellions that troubled the early years of her son's reign.

Louis undertook two crusades, and his standards of chivalry and justice closely approximated the medieval ideal of what kingship ought to be. His younger friend and comrade-in-arms, Jean de Joinville, wrote a famous biography of the king. From the selection included in this book, it is clear that Joinville was impressed by St. Louis' moral standards and sense of fair play. Does this selection not reveal as much about Joinville and his class as it may about the king? To promote peace among Christians, Louis was prepared to make compromises that some modern nationalist historians have criticized as contrary to the best interests of the monarchy. Fawtier, however, has argued that Louis' strong sense of the rightness and majesty of the crown contributed, in its own way, to the development of absolutism.

St. Louis left his successors a valuable legacy of moral prestige, but they found it hard to live up to his standards as the peaceful and prosperous thirteenth century gave way to more troubled times. His grandson, Philip IV, called the Fair, clashed with the pope, the count of Flanders, and the English in the course of a stormy reign; as will be seen below, his career remains a subject of great debate.

The century from Philip II to Philip IV was marked by a vast increase in the royal domain and the growth of population, towns, and commerce. These economic changes favored larger political units but also required more elaborate political institutions. The early development of these institutions is the subject of the three selections in Part IV. James Fesler examines local administration, stressing the relationship of the central government to the bailiffs and seneschals. These were salaried officials serving short terms in charge of the thirty-odd districts into which the domain was divided by the end of the thirteenth century.

From Fesler's description, the government would seem to have been increasingly centralized under the direction of Paris, but Jan Rogozinski presents a different perspective. Legal customs varied from one part of France to another, and, according to Rogozinski, the seneschals sent to Languedoc depended heavily on local persons trained in the law of their particular region. Important southern lawyers, serving as royal judges, helped to perpetuate distinctive local traditions.

If the practices of the lawyer class tended to favor regional differences, what are we to conclude about the progress of royal centralization in the thirteenth century?

There were, in fact, other kinds of law which had a more favorable effect on centralization because of their universal character. These were Roman civil law and the canon law of the Church. The crown made increasing use of legists trained in these two laws, and Franklin Pegues has studied their role in the central government in the period around 1300. He argues that their main purpose was to enhance royal finances and that the most important royal lawyers adopted the practice of going into the field to supervise personally the execution of policies established in Paris.

Pegues takes issue with earlier historians of the reign of Philip the Fair. It was once suggested that this king was actually a nonentity and that policy was in the hands of unscrupulous legal advisers of bourgeois origins who sought to destroy the feudal nobility and create an absolute monarchy. Pegues concludes that many of these men were nobles, that all had noble clients, and that they served a king whose purpose was not to establish a dictatorship but only to obtain more money.

The enigma of Philip the Fair is considered in Part V. While stressing that Philip was no mere figurehead, Joseph Strayer describes him as a constitutional monarch precisely because he did rely on advisers in accordance with medieval custom. Bryce Lyon, on the other hand, denies that Philip can be called a constitutional king merely because he sought advice. According to Lyon, Philip did not have to face the sort of political pressures which alone could force a monarch to act in a constitutional fashion.

An entirely different view is presented by Elizabeth Brown. While agreeing with Pegues and others that royal lawyers developed theories calculated to expand royal fiscal power, she suggests that Philip was equally influenced by the warnings of the theologians against extortion. It is her view that the king had to contend not only with political pressures but also with his own conscience, and his actions proved to be politically short-sighted. The result was that he left his successors with diminished authority in the financial sphere.

The royal need for added revenues was related to the increased level of warfare. By the end of the thirteenth century, the European monarchies had consolidated their power. Their lofty ambitions and restive nobles helped create international conflicts that their inadequate fiscal institutions could not sustain, and the problem grew worse as the economy deteriorated during the fourteenth century. The troubles of Philip IV, depicted by Brown, foreshadowed the graver difficulties encountered by Philip's successors. Frenchmen did not appear deeply concerned about the right to consent to taxation, for they would pay to defend the realm in any manifest emergency. They were unwilling to pay, however, once the emergency was over, and they would not always accept the king's definition of an emergency. The threat had to be obvious at the local level, a war with actual fighting.

Facing military, fiscal, and economic problems, the crown continued to develop the sort of institutions needed for a strong state, but their growth was slow and much of the process is still obscure. Assemblies of barons, prelates, and town representatives, later known as the Estates General, were convened occasionally by the early fourteenth-century kings for propaganda purposes. When consulted on fiscal matters, they were willing to give counsel about whether an emergency justified taxation but not to give consent to a specific tax binding on their constituents. Royal revenues were still mostly feudal or seigneurial in origin, and their collection was supervised by a body called the Chamber of Accounts. Special war subsidies, more like taxes in the modern sense, became increasingly frequent, but they still were regarded as extraordinary, and there was not yet a permanent administration to deal with them.

Part VI deals with the crises of the fourteenth and fifteenth centuries. The crown's growing concern with finances made the Chamber of Accounts extremely influential in the reign of Philip VI (r. 1328-1350). According to Raymond Cazelles, the president, or "sovereigns" of this body became virtually identical with the king's council in the decade after 1335. Their ascendancy aroused jealousies, however, and rivals soon appeared in the *Parlement,* or supreme judicial court. The members of this court could appeal to the memory of St. Louis and the tradition of royal justice, whereas financial officers always made convenient scapegoats when things went wrong.

Following a military defeat in 1346, the Chamber of Accounts was divorced from the royal council, and the crown began exploring new ways of administering extraordinary taxes. The Estates were asked to grant taxes that would be collected by their own appointees (*élus*). After several unsuccessful efforts in this direction, the Estates General lost prestige and went into eclipse, and a new administration was set up during the 1360s without help from central assemblies. In that decade, the monarchy established regular peacetime taxes for the first time: sales taxes, called *aides* and *gabelles,* which were to pay the ransom of the captured king John II; and a hearth tax (known as the *taille* in the fifteenth century) which was to pay for defensive measures against brigands. These were all collected by royal *élus* supervised by a board of *généraux*, which became known as the Court of the Aids. The Chamber of Accounts, now confined to administering domainal revenues of declining importance, suffered a long eclipse, and from 1345 onwards the *Parlement* regained an influence it would enjoy for centuries.

These institutional and political changes occurred during a period of general crisis in France. For the monarchy, this crisis was dominated by a succession dispute, which is briefly described in the selection by Cazelles. In 1316, for the first time in twelve generations, the throne was left without a direct male heir. Louis X's young daughter was excluded from the throne, which passed successively to Louis's two brothers, the younger sons of Philip the Fair. When they also died without sons, the question was reopened in 1328. Philip IV's only grandson was the sixteen-year-old Plantagenet king of England, Edward III. Cazelles suggests some reasons why the French rejected Edward's claim and conferred the crown on Philip of Valois (Philip VI), nephew of Philip IV. Henceforth it was held that women could not transmit claims to the French throne.

Whatever the wisdom of this decision, it made Philip VI the prisoner of those who had made him king, and it left nagging doubts about his legitimacy. Edward III, who had other grievances against France, soon reasserted his claim to the throne, and in 1337 the Hundred Years' War began. Not only did the Valois monarchy suffer military defeat, but the war coincided with other catastrophes: economic decline, recurrent plagues, schism in the Church, and destructive brigandage by undisciplined soldiery.

In this atmosphere of general crisis, can we point to any one factor as decisive? For Peter S. Lewis, the disputed succession was fundamental. The French monarchy was no longer buttressed by the almost sacred legitimacy of the Capetian house. The uncertain right of the Valois gave rebels and malcontents an excellent opportunity to swear allegiance to an alternative dynasty. The strains created by this situation are illustrated by Edouard Perroy's characterization of Philip VI's successor, John II (r. 1350-1364), who "lived in a permanent state of panic." The monarchy made a brief military and financial recovery in the 1370s under John's able successor Charles V, and the achievements of that period were given permanence seventy years later under Charles VII. In between these kings, however, France experienced calamities that brought the Valois monarchy to the nadir of its fortunes. In 1392 Charles VI went insane, and for thirty years the princes and lords plundered the treasury, fought each other, and left the kingdom helpless before a strong new English advance. Lewis has gone so far as to argue that the entire Hundred Years' War may be regarded as a civil war between factions of the still untamed aristocracy.

In the end, Lewis feels, the Valois kings could claim the victory, as the great feudal princes were subdued and the English driven from the continent. This triumph, however, like the earlier achievements of Philip II, was not accomplished without some good fortune. The teen-age mystic, St. Joan of Arc, played a brief but inspirational role in 1429-30. Several important princely families died out at opportune moments. Finally, the English were weakened in the mid-fifteenth century by the civil strife of their own feudal princes. Lewis discusses the foibles and eccentricities of the Valois kings of France but concludes that some had real ability. Louis XI (r. 1461-1483), for all his peculiarities, knew how to exploit his opportunities to the best advantage.

From the reign of Eudes to that of Louis XI, six centuries elapsed, and more than two dozen kings reigned in France. If none of them showed real genius, they certainly displayed a multitude of other characteristics. Among them were generals, administrators, and politicians, a madman, and a saint. All of them, after the eleventh century, were believed able to cure a disease by their touch. During those six centuries, France developed institutions and governmental traditions that survived until 1789 and, in some cases, are present today.

Yet, as the following selections suggest, many questions about these six centuries are still to be resolved. To what extent did the "great" kings profit from the work of dedicated servants or less heralded predecessors? How effectively did the medieval monarchy build a unified state? What is to be our final judgment of Philip the Fair? Perhaps the ultimate question for students to consider is the degree to which the monarchy actually shaped the development of the French nation.

In the reprinted selections, footnotes appearing in the original sources have in general been omitted unless they contribute to the argument or better the understanding of the selection.

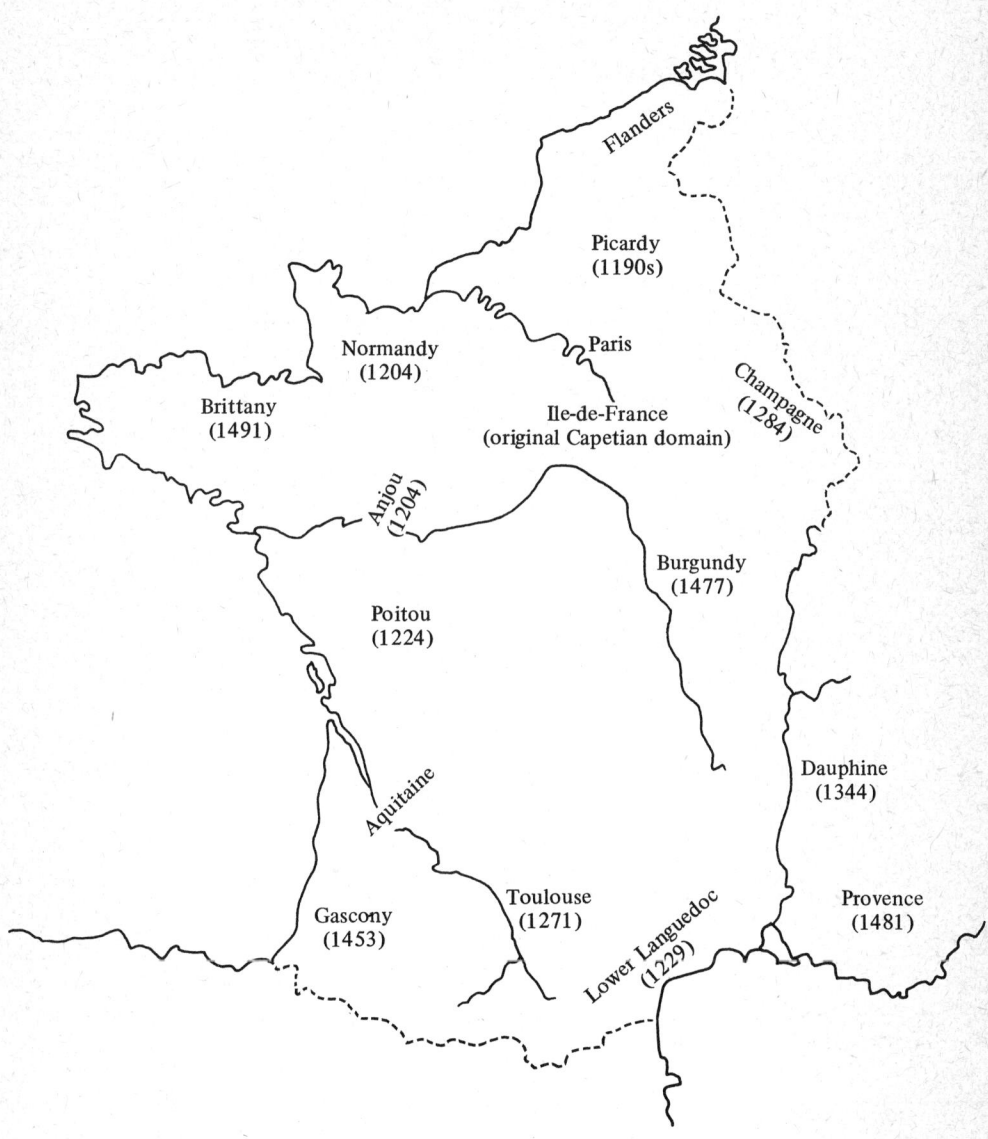

MEDIEVAL FRANCE
Principal regions and dates at which they became part of royal domain.

KINGS OF MEDIEVAL FRANCE

Carolingian Family
Pepin 751-768
Carloman I 768-771
Charles I (Charlemagne) 768-814
Louis I (the Pious) 814-840
Charles II (the Bald) 840-877
Louis II (the Stammerer) 877-879
Louis III 879-882
Carloman II 879-884
(884-887: Reunited to German Empire under Charles the Fat)
Charles III (the Simple) 898-922
Louis IV (the Exile) 936-954
Lothair I 954-986
Louis V 986-987

Robertian or Capetian Family
Eudes 887-898
Robert I 922-923
Raoul 923-936
Hugh Capet 987-996
Robert II (the Pious) 996-1031

Henry I 1031-1060
Philip I (the Fat) 1060-1108
Louis VI (the Fat) 1108-1137
Louis VII (the Young) 1137-1180
Philip II (Augustus) 1180-1223
Louis VIII 1223-1226
Louis IX (the Saint) 1226-1270
Philip III (the Bold) 1270-1285
Philip IV (the Fair) 1285-1314
Louis X (the Headstrong) 1314-1316
John I (Posthumous) 1316
Philip V (the Tall) 1316-1322
Charles IV (the Fair) 1322-1328

Valois Family
Philip VI 1328-1350
John II (the Good) 1350-1364
Charles V (the Wise) 1364-1380
Charles VI (the Mad) 1380-1422
Charles VII (the Well-Served) 1422-1461
Louis XI (the Spider) 1461-1483
Charles VIII 1483-1498

THE VALOIS SUCCESSION

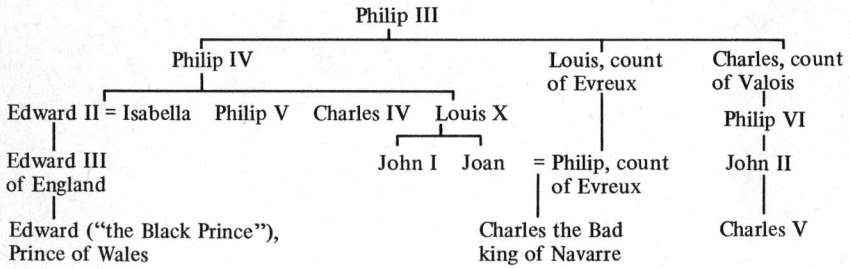

Part One: DISINTEGRATION OF THE CAROLINGIAN MONARCHY

Chapter 1 NATIONALISM AND THE TERRITORIAL PRINCIPALITIES

The medieval French monarchy was created when Charlemagne's empire was divided among his grandsons in 843. Scarcely a generation passed, however, before the West Frankish kingdom itself began to disintegrate, and power became regional in character. JAN DHONDT (b. 1915), professor at the University of Ghent, has devoted years of study to this process, concentrating on the county of Flanders. His major synthesis, from which this excerpt is taken, deals with the emergence of territorial principalities in France and the role of non-Frankish peoples in their formation.

The history of France in the ninth and tenth centuries is characterized, not . . . by the replacement of the Carolingian dynasty by the Capetian, but by the elimination of centralized monarchy to the benefit of territorial princes. In fact, a political framework that was not only obsolete and worn out at the moment of its disappearance, but also anachronistic from its very birth, was [now] replaced by other forms better adapted to the conditions of their epoch. That the territorial principalities were in harmony with their times, we need no other proof than their longevity: up to the dawn of the thirteenth century they had formed the basis for the political existence of France, and the sovereign himself had importance only

From Jan Dhondt, *Etudes sur la naissance des principautés territoriales en France* (Bruges: Uitgeverij De Tempel, 1948), pp. 231-232, 234-236, 238-240, 243-244. Reprinted by permission of the author. Translated by John B. Henneman.

insofar as he was a territorial prince. For a long time thereafter they survived and remained an essential factor. Carolingian royalty, on the other hand, barely held its own for a century.

Even more noteworthy is the fact that although the establishment of a territorial principality supposes a profound revolution by which the totality of power in a given region passes from the hands of the king into the hands of one of his subjects, this revolution took place over several decades, and not sporadically but in all of France, in Germany, in Italy; in a word, in the whole empire. Thus it was not a question of local accidents but of a general phenomenon whose origin must have been related to the essential characteristics of the Carolingian state. Why did the empire that Pepin and Charlemagne founded collapse so quickly and so completely? It is that its very creation constituted an anachronism, a monstrous attempt to turn back to an outdated past. Pepin believed that it was possible to restore the kingship for his own benefit, on the condition that he had the disposal of what the last descendants of Clovis had lacked, the lands necessary to buy indispensable support. Nothing was more false; the very conditions of the age condemned all great centralized states to perish. It did not suffice to depose the Merovingians in order to reign effectively.

Unlike the Merovingians when they established their power, the Pippinids did not enjoy the prestige of a conqueror, the support of a recognized authority such as divine origin, and the centralizing traditions introduced by the Romans. They either had to perish or to build from scratch an administrative system capable of transforming their vast but heterogeneous state into a coherent whole. In effect, the Carolingian empire consisted of a veritable conglomerate of diverse nationalities who kept alive the sense of their individuality and tried incessantly to escape the Frankish enterprise. Nothing demonstrates this fact better than the history of Aquitaine . . .

What does not appear contestable with respect to the Aquitanians is also neither contestable nor contested with respect to other populations of the Carolingian empire. No one cares to deny the persistence, throughout the Carolingian era, of a Breton, Gascon, Gothic, Saxon, or Bavarian nationality. In conclusion, we may consider as established the existence of nationalities, of ethnic groups, in the Carolingian period.

We have no thought, however, of attributing to men of the ninth century the sentiments of the twentieth. We do not believe that the contemporaries of Charlemagne, illiterate, sedentary, confined in a restricted region, had an active, powerful sense of their national conscience. But what cannot be denied . . . is an instinctive distrust, approaching hostility, for those who did not belong to their own community, who did not speak their language, who did not have the same habits of life. Now in all parts of the empire it was the Frank who was the foreigner or, what is worse, the conqueror. And it is thus probable that from the Ebro to the Elbe the same desire to throw off the Carolingian yoke vaguely existed.

To maintain their authority over these non-Frankish nationalities who populated the greater part of the empire, Pepin and his descendents necessarily had to rely on Franks, that is to say, in the Carolingian period, the inhabitants of *Francia,* between the Loire and the Rhine. At the same time, their own authority over these people was limited by the influence exercised in the Frankish lands by the great landed proprietors. The Carolingians themselves had come from this landed class; it was as heads of the aristocracy that they had begun the struggle against the Merovingians. Since then they had risen above their peers. Had the latter borne no grudge? We do not know, but it is evident that the Carolingians had every interest in living on good terms with these people whose influence among the Franks must have been very great. The sovereigns also endeavored to align the cause of the great landed families closely to their own. In lavishing favors on them, they persuaded the magnates to enter into Carolingian vassalage and even to occupy posts in the administration. In practice, the comital dignities were reserved for members of families of the Frankish aristocracy. This is to say that the members of these families were directly interested in maintaining the Frankish domination over the alien nationalities. In effect, the important revenue of the comital office and the enjoyment of the vast *"res de comitatu"*[1] were a function of the recognition of royal authority by the subject populations. A foreigner, and one isolated in the middle of a hostile population, the great proprietor-turned-administrator of a *pagus* had no recourse other than the crown in time of grave troubles. This was just what the Carolingians wished, and the whole policy of the sovereign aimed at preventing the count from creating for himself an independent position in his county. To this end a severe control over his activity was exercised by the *missi dominici*; rival powers to those of the count were set up in the interior of the countries, the *vassi dominici* and lay abbots; finally, and especially, the counts were moved about as frequently as possible.

But the economic structure of the age resisted the mobility of officials. The latter profited from their positions to acquire estates in their county, either arrogating to themselves the property of the fisc [royal lands] or exercising pressure on the landowners to induce them to give up their property. The establishment of a landed domain attached the count in some way to a definite region, leading him to resist his displacement, to anchor himself in his county. Thus it is clear that the great comital dynasties, nearly all ... originally from Austrasia, established themselves successively in one or another region of France ...

The establishment of comital power ... prevented the sovereign from defeating the opposition of the counts to their displacement; soon the comital careers would be characterized by a real stability. Simultaneously, as the Carolingian power diminished, the palace's agents of control, the *missi dominici,* were losing their importance. The sovereign soon gave up the vital privilege of choosing them himself and allowed the intervention of the magnates in this operation. Subsequently, the itinerant and annual *missi* would be replaced by *missi* chosen from among the great men of the region which they had to supervise, which is to say that their control [over these local magnates] became illusory . . .

The practice of accumulating counties, which triumphed in the time of Charles the Bald (r. 840-877), reinforced the personal position of the count, whose resources increased in proportion to the extent of the territory he administered. In the second half of the reign of Charles the Bald, a certain imbalance between the central authority and that of the counts began to emerge. The counts gave proof of their insubordination, persecuted the *vassi dominici,* tried to influence episcopal elections for their own ends when they were supposed to intervene only to defend the king's interest. . . . In sum, the use of great Frankish landowners to contain the non-Frankish populations ended in catastrophe. These persons, previously merely great landowners, were invested by the king with public authority. And, in addition, their power was further increased formidably by the masses of land from the fisc that the crown was progressively induced to grant them, the immune abbeys of which they became lay abbots, and all that was made possible by the king's abandonment of his rights and revenues. . . .

After this phase came another, during which the magnates—that is, the foremost counts, whose origin, alliances, and personal qualities put them in the first rank— secured for themselves, in defiance of the king, all the elements of power and set to work to create an independent state. At this point there developed an undeniable *rapprochement* between nationalities and magnates, and it is from this reconciliation that the territorial principality developed.

This *rapprochement* was, in fact, inevitable. Having become great landed proprietors in the regions they administered, the Frankish counts had important interests in common with those they ruled. Obliged for the pursuit of their particular ends, to collect vassals, they could recruit them only in the regions where their domains lay, whose populations were generally non-Frankish; hence a new and solid tie. Finally, becoming aware of the possibility of total independence in the face of the continued weakening of royal power, the magnate seeking support against the crown could not neglect to utilize the aspirations of the nationalities.

The progressive weakening of royal power, the *rapprochement* of the representatives of Carolingian power with the populations desiring to free themselves from Carolingian authority, the reinforcing of the nationalities' tendency toward autonomy, and the decentralizing tendencies of the great landed dynasties [were factors that] could only lead to the dislocation of the Carolingian monarchy. But with what could it be replaced? It is clear that at the end of the reign of Charles the Bald nobody knew. It was after various attempts and experiences that the formula of the territorial principality was developed . . .

Thus the trend of usurpation had began very soon. When was it completed? All we can say is that after the reign of Eudes (887-898) the interventions of the crown in different parts of France, still rather frequent before his accession to the throne, became excessively rare in Aquitaine and in Burgundy. Besides, we are certain that in the tenth and eleventh centuries all the rights in these countries remained in the hands of the territorial princes . . . In France Minor the royalty maintained itself better; in fact, it always kept a few scattered rights in the region, which did not prevent the authority of the territorial princes [there] from being almost as strong in 987 as in Aquitaine and Burgundy.

Is it from the time of Eudes that we must date the formation of the territorial principalities? It is a reasonable assumption, because it was precisely during this time that the territorial outlines were established which later became principalities. During these very years, Baldwin II created the Flemish state, and Richard the Lawgiver built the duchy of Burgundy. From the odd collection of the counties of Bernard Plantevelue were born the first duchy of Aquitaine of [Bernard's] son William the Pious and the March of Toulouse.[2] And it was around 900, finally, that the Neustrian provincipality was born, and the Norman state was built. We cannot affirm that from this moment all the powers in the interior of the new districts devolved upon the prince, but it is certain that he already possessed a part of them and that they all would be in his hands eventually.

Notes

1. Royal lands and revenues attached to the office, or *honor*, of count and providing the holder of the office with a salary. [Ed.].

2. The March was a group of counties, usually along a border, placed under the control of an important military commander, usually called a duke or marquis. According to Dhondt, the accumulation of several counties into a March was the most common way of building a territorial principality [Ed.].

Chapter 2 THE FAILURE OF PUBLIC AUTHORITY IN LANGUEDOC

ARCHIBALD R. LEWIS (b. 1914), now a professor at the University of Massachusetts after a long career at the University of Texas, is a leading American historian of the early middle ages. He has written books on early medieval trade and naval power in the North Sea, the Baltic, and the Mediterranean, and a synthesis entitled *Emerging Medieval Europe* (New York: Alfred A. Knopf, 1967.) The selection here is taken from a volume on the social history of southern France in which he challenges some of Dhondt's conclusions about the rise of territorial principalities.

The last years of the reign of Louis the Pious saw the beginning of a period of disorder which was to affect most regions of Southern France and the Spanish March for some seven decades. By the end of this period royal authority had all but vanished over the lands which lay south of Poitou and Burgundy. A new order of things had emerged in which real, *de facto* power had passed into the hands of a series of noble families who, by hereditary right, ruled local areas and were powerful enough to ignore the royal government.

The story of the emergence of such independent local ruling families is a complex one, and historians are still very much in disagreement over the details which

From Archibald R. Lewis, *The Development of Southern French and Catalan Society, 718-1050* (Austin, 1965), pp. 91-92, 111-113, 179-181, 185, 195-197, 210-211, 214, 217-219. Reprinted by permission of the University of Texas Press. Most of the author's footnotes omitted.

attended the process and even, in some respects, over basic causes. It does, however, seem to be agreed that this change was due to a series or combination of factors. Perhaps the most important one was the civil strife which continued intermittently among various members of the Carolingian royal house and then between them and the rising Capetian family. Almost equally important as a basic factor were invasions by Vikings and Moslems which proved the inability of the royal government to protect its realm. Finally there was the policy of elevating certain officials to great authority by giving them command over two or more counties of the empire which, more often than not, resulted in their disloyalty to the central authorities as they attempted to make themselves completely independent.

All three of these factors were, as a matter of fact, interrelated. Dissension within the empire and civil war encouraged outside attack. Danger along the frontiers and actual invasions made it necessary to give broad powers over wide areas to certain counts. Such officials increased their authority still further by playing one side against the other in the disputes which the various heirs of Louis the Pious had with one another. They could even negotiate or ally themselves with foreign invaders. Finally they could become powerful enough to revolt openly, which encouraged invaders and started the whole cycle going again.

Faced by this dangerous cycle Carolingian rulers strove to maintain their authority by maintaining peace, whenever possible, along their frontiers and by delicately balancing the power of their dangerous subordinates, the counts, by removing some from office and playing the rest one against the other as the occasion demanded. The remarkable thing is that they succeeded in maintaining their authority as long as they did ... Yet in each crisis they were forced to give up a little more royal authority to gain support, until by the time of Charles the Fat they had little power left. When Eudes, of the new Capetian family, became king late in the century, he found himself a monarch who possessed only shadowy rights south of Poitou and Burgundy. An old era had ended and a new one was at hand ...

Now when we come to analyze these twelve families who by the year 900 had come to exercise ruling authority over Southern France and the Spanish March by hereditary right a number of things seem apparent to us. First of all we are struck by the fact that all of them, with the exception of the dukes of Gascony, gained a real and *de facto* independence between the years 870 and 890, a period which comprised the last years of Charles the Bald, the three short reigns of his Carolingian successors, and the first years of King Eudes of the Capetian line. It was during these two decades that Northern French monarchs lost effective control over the Midi and Catalonia.

Furthermore, we can mark the steps in this process. The murder of Count Bernard of Toulouse and the taking over of his *honores* by Bernard Plantevelue in 872, followed as it was by the loss of Pallars and Ribagorça, seems to be the first step. The famous Assembly of Quiersy in 877 where the magnates protected their rights of succession to their *honores* seems a second.[1] The deprivation of the *honores* of Bernard of Gothia in 879 by the magnates and their redistribution seems a third step. Finally, after the disastrous reign of Charles the Fat, the accession of Eudes represented the final step, since the lords of the Midi could, by claiming a Carolingian loyalty, in effect make themselves independent. This is just what they did. Out of civil wars, rebellions, invasions, and royal weakness, then, there developed a group of noble families who now ruled south of Burgundy and Poitou by hereditary *de facto* right.

Examination of these families, however, shows us more than this fact, well known to historians. For though all of them, except the Gascon dukes, owed their *final* independence to the events of the years 870-890, the circumstances which led each family to establish itself firmly in the local district varied immensely. One family, the Gascon dukes, goes back to the pre-Carolingian period. All the other eleven were initially appointed to power over the region or regions they came to rule by Carolingian monarchs . . . But the dates when they began to establish themselves in their regions vary immensely. Four began to establish themselves during the reigns of Charlemagne, and the first years of Louis the Pious—the family of Melgueil, that of Carcassonne, that of the Bernards of Auvergne, that of Ademar of Poitou. Four others seem to date from the very last years of Louis the Pious and the early years of the reign of Charles the Bald—the family of Toulouse, that of Rannoux of Poitou, and those of Ampurias-Rousillon and Urgell-Cerdanya-Besalu. Three became firmly established in their regions very late—that of Vulgrin of Angoulême-Périgord that of Ramón of Pallars-Ribagorça, and that of Boson of Provence. Viewed in this way then, the development of independent ruling families in these regions was a slow, evolutionary process in some cases, a rapid affair in others—dependent on the special and varied circumstances which affected every family quite differently. Such facts seem to preclude any sudden revolutionary forces at work in the process, such as some historians have seemed to emphasize.

Even more interesting is an analysis of the nationalities represented by these families. As far as we can tell, one was Gascon, one Hispano-Gascon, three Gothic, six Frankish, and one either Frankish or Gallo-Roman.[2] In the case of the Gascon dukes, their support may have been due to a dislike of alien Frankish rule. In the case of the others we have no reason or facts upon which we can base such an opinion. In fact, the last two families who managed to establish themselves in our regions, those of Vulgrin and Boson, were Frankish ones who established their authority in areas which were overwhelmingly Gallo-Roman in character. Even a nascent nationalism, except in Gascony, is hard to discern as a cause of the failure of the Carolingians to maintain their authority over Southern France and Catalonia.

To sum up then, civil wars and invasions weakened the imperfect system of centralized control which the Carolingians had established in Southern France and the Spanish March. Special circumstances, the most important being the short reigns of Charles the Bald's successors and the accession of King Eudes allowed the leading ruling counts of the Midi and Catalonia to establish their families as hereditary and independent *in fact* of royal authority. This, however, more often than not, was the result of no sudden, revolutionary situation, but the culmination of a slow, gradual evolution of authority which, for most of these families, took many decades. This process, inevitable under the circumstances, rather than any supposed national consciousness of portions of the Midi and the Spanish March explains in large measure the new situation which by 900 had arisen out of the failures and weaknesses of the Carolingians.[3] . . .

By the first years of the tenth century Frankish monarchs who lived north of the Loire had lost all effective control over Southern France and Catalonia. Real authority over the Spanish March, Gascony, Septimania, Aquitaine and the Valley of the Rhone was now in the hands of noble families, who, by hereditary right, seem to have exercised such functions of government as remained and who tended to dominate the Church as well. This end of the power of the royal government, however, did not destroy all vestiges of influence which French monarchs still exercised over these regions. Some remained down to the middle of the tenth century and even afterwards, until it disappeared, not to be found again until the middle of the twelfth century.

Let us examine this ending of royal influence over the Midi and Catalonia and the reasons for it. We might perhaps best begin by considering the matter of royal presence in these regions. From 900 on our evidence seems to show that kings of France rarely traveled south of Poitou and Burgundy. When they did, they seem to have confined their visits to regions like Auvergne and Western Aquitaine which were close to their northern centers of authority. Of all these kings, Raoul seems to have shown the most interest in the Midi, traveling to LePuy and Auvergne and acting for a period in a military capacity in the Limousin, Quercy, and adjoining regions. Louis IV probably made several visits to Western Aquitaine and Auvergne. Lothaire certainly visited LePuy. In contrast to a Charles the Bald or a Carolman, however, northern French rulers seem to have showed little direct interest in their southern domains, if by interest one means actual visits.

We have, however, other indices of interest, besides actual visits, which need to be examined. That is evidence of charters issued by these rulers which concern the Midi and Catalonia and are proof of continuing ties of homage or *fidelitas,* which linked important noble families of these regions to a distant crown. Before examining these two points, however, we must emphasize that there were at least two regions of Southern France and the Spanish March in which neither of these two forms of continued royal influences are to be found in this period. I refer to the Valley of the Rhone and to Pallars and Ribagorça. The Valley of the Rhone, after 890, had kings of its own and so did not recognize, even in theory, northern French monarchs, while Pallars and Ribagorça from the late ninth century on had counts who both in theory and in fact possessed power independent of the kings who lived north of the Loire.

Elsewhere, however, charters and evidence of homage seem to point out that some royal influence remained in most regions south of Poitou and Burgundy down into the reign of Lothaire. Lest we overestimate the importance of this influence, however, we need to understand its true basis and nature in the light of the political realities of the period. The first of these political realities was the rivalry which existed between the older Carolingian family and the new rising power of the Capetians. This rivalry led to a practice of choosing monarchs alternately from these rival houses ... Louis IV reestablished his family in control of the monarchy for most of the rest of the century until the Capetians finally won out permanently at the time of Hugh Capet.

This rivalry was one in which the noble families of the Midi and Catalonia could take very little part, even if they had wished to do so. Election of monarchs seems to have been a prerogative of Northern French magnates and churchmen, who encouraged Capetian-Carolingian rivalry since this forced each monarch to bid for their support with important concessions. But it did have serious political effects upon the magnates who controlled political power south of Poitou and Burgundy.

Much more important for the Midi and Catalonia during this period, though, was another rivalry-one which involved the House of Toulouse and neighboring noble families ... The House of Toulouse and its allies controlled a wide belt of territory during this period, which effectively separated their northern enemies in Poitou and Auvergne from their southern adversaries in Carcassonne-Razés and Catalonia. In the continuing struggle both sides found royal influence a useful weapon, just as both the Carolingians and Capetians sought the support of these same powerful magnates in the course of their own rivalry ...

The story of the decline and disappearance of royal authority and influence in Southern France and Catalonia brings up a most important question. What took its place beyond such influence as could be exerted by the Papacy, Cluny, and the caliphs of Cordova? Were the important noble families who emerged as masters of local regions and the local Church able, as a result, to create principalities on the bones of a decayed Carolingian system? Such seems to be the contention of a recent historian who has examined this question and who appears to postulate such a development as all but automatic.[4] Yet there is little evidence that he is correct. The fact seems to be instead that when Carolingian royal control of the Midi and the Spanish March ended in the last years of the ninth century, the leading magnates were unable to create territorial states in its place, despite all efforts to do so.

What then did happen? The story of the first three quarters of the tenth century is one not of the success but of the failure of the territorial state in these regions, and of a continuing decay of such machinery of government as survived—except perhaps in Catalonia which in many ways presents a unique situation. By 975 what had emerged in Southern France was not principalities, but a system which was so disorganized in a political sense that it approached anarchy—an anarchy that only slowly began to develop into a more orderly pattern of government.

Perhaps the best way to make clear this continuing decay of governmental organization and the failure of organized principalities to emerge is to examine our regions in 900 and contrast them with the situation to be found in 975. At the earlier date, as we have already emphasized, political authority had moved from the Northern French monarchs into the hands of a group of noble families. One of these had assumed a royal title and controlled the general region of the Rhone Valley. The other eleven dominated the rest of Southern France and the Spanish March as counts—two in Septimania, three in Catalonia, one in Gascony, and four in Aquitaine. Assisting them and sharing a measure of authority with them were a number of viscounts who had already made their appearance . . .

What do we find by 975? We find that the number of independent comital and viscontal families has multiplied, until we can list some hundred and fifty who hold their authority by hereditary right. In some regions . . . these families are so numerous that it is all but impossible to disentangle them or to discover with any accuracy their origins. . . . The number of families in positions of authority had so multiplied in most of the Midi that the age of the *princeps* [prince] had become the period of the *principes* [princes]. Nor does the above suffice in explaining the extent of the diffusion of political power. For we must add to such secular ruling families ecclesiastical magnates as well; bishops like those of Limoges, Angoulême, Le Puy, and Grenoble, or archbishops like those of Lyon, Vienne, and Narbonne. Such churchmen during this period were often the almost unchallenged masters of large parts of the Midi.

How did this decay and fragmentation of principalities come about? Why were families who controlled important portions of the Midi and Catalonia in 900 unable to create any form of principality—feudal or nonfeudal, which was capable of resisting progressive disintegration? And what happened to the governmental system of the Midi and the Spanish March as a result of such failures? These are the questions which demand answers. One might approach the answers in various ways, but perhaps a good method is to concentrate on a certain number of the ruling families who appear to have controlled the Midi and Catalonia in 900, and to trace their history and that of the regions where they were powerful down to 975 . . .

Examination of the leading families of the Midi and the Spanish March makes it clear that no principalities arose to take the place of Carolingian government. But it leaves unanswered the basic question as to why this was so. The first and most important reason we can give has to do with the operation of the family system in Southern France and Catalonia . . . By 900, families had become the controlling element in government, as they took over what in Carolingian times had been *honores*. During the first generation or so family solidarity tended to preserve a certain unity in regions which a particular family controlled . . . But eventually the principle of *divisio* and the habit of allowing widows to continue to control their husbands' estates triumphed over family unity . . . The tendency of land granted to *fideles* to become allodial[5] was a feature of this period, and one which must bear a large share of the responsibility, along with the workings of the family system, for the failure to develop territorial states south of Poitou and Burgundy . . .

As governmental authority and forms decayed still further in most of our regions . . . the destiny of the Midi was to see . . . unusual tribunals . . . Such courts were not feudal, but rather seem to have been informal gatherings of leading landowners and churchmen of a particular region, who met together to decide matters which earlier in Carolingian times had come before a *mallus publicus*[6] . . . Groups of *boni homines* deriving their authority from their habit of attending the public courts and their use as witnesses to private agreements and family charters began to informally assume the right to judge disputes concerning land, where no other clear jurisdiction existed. Since the authority of these *boni homines* and others who met informally in such assemblies rested essentially upon public opinion, they strove to arbitrate disputes rather than use force, but this does not mean they were without power. They had a great deal, and continued to use it in this period and later on . . . And their verdicts had the force of law through their very importance. The fate of the Carolingian legal system in the Midi, then, was not to disappear into feudalized courts, but to disappear and to be replaced by assemblies of important landholders and church magnates who rendered such rough justice as was possible under the circumstances and who kept disorders to a minimum at a time when there was little judicial authority upon which society could depend.

Notes

1. The Assembly of Quiersy did not make all *honores* hereditary, only those assigned to the magnates who were accompanying Charles the Bald on his Italian campaign . . . On the other hand, it did help to serve as a precedent for making all other *honores* hereditary too.

2. The dukes of Gascony were of Gascon origin; the counts of Carcassonne, Ampurias, and Barcelona were Gothic; the counts of Melgueil, Toulouse, Auvergne, Angoulême, and Poitou and the kings of Provence-Burgundy were Frankish; the counts of Pallars and Ribagorça were Hispano-Basque; and the counts of Périgord were either Frankish or Gallo-Roman.

3. Both Calmette and Dhondt have emphasized nationalities as a cause of the disintegration of Carolingian rule in the Midi and Catalonia . . . [But] the major problem of the period was not an incipient nationalism but a split between the powerful landowners and the less powerful mass of the population . . . If we add a split between the crown and magnates, we have a real explanation of what happened to the Carolingian Empire in this part of France and Catalonia.

4. See J. Dhondt, *études sur la naissance des principautés territorialés en France,* for an expression of this point of view. In this work, Dhondt makes the assumption, without proof, that the decline of royal power *automatically* made for principalities.

5. Allodial land was owned outright, as opposed to fiefs and other forms of tenure, in which the occupant of the land did not own it but had possession of it subject ot certain rents or services to the owner.[Ed.]

6. The county court of Carolingian times had called the *mallus publicus.* [Ed.]

Part Two: CHANGE OF DYNASTY IN 987

Chapter 3 THE CONTRACTING SPHERE OF ROYAL INFLUENCE

JEAN-FRANCOIS LEMARIGNIER (b. 1913), a distinguished scholar of the early middle ages, has made important recent contributions to medieval French historiography. He has made a special study of the evolution and expansion of monasticism in the tenth and eleventh centuries and the acts of the first Capetian kings in this same period. This excerpt and the one in Part III are taken from Lemarignier's masterly study of the diplomas and charters of these kings, from which he drew important new conclusions about the changing character of royal power.

The accession of Hugh Capet in 987 has contradictory significance. On the one hand, it is certain that its continuation exaggerated its importance. In the eyes of many contemporaries it fitted into the pattern of alternating kingship between Carolingians and Robertians, of which the century just completed had given several examples, at least in the first half. And, in certain respects, there was no pause in the history of kingship, [so that] Ferdinand Lot, who has studied it best, could speak of its "insignificance." It nevertheless remains—this is the second aspect—that it marked the end of an attempt at a Carolingian restoration, which had just gone on for half a century and had enabled the last three kings of the former dynasty to succeed each other from father to son. The third of them, Louis V, had to die quite

From Jean-François Lemarignier, *Le gouvernement royal aux premiers temps capétiens (987-1108)* (Paris, 1965) pp. 37-38, 40-43, 46-47, 55-56, 58, 67-70, 72. Reprinted by permission of Editions A. et J. Picard et Cie. Translated by John B. Henneman and Rosalie A. Vermette.

young and childless before the kingship could be given to Hugh in the absence of an heir of the direct line, a sign of the prestige that the line of Charlemagne still enjoyed in this western kingdom that had been its last refuge. This prestige, joined to the sense of legitimacy which still sustained it, was lacking in the new dynasty. From this [occurred] the struggles that Hugh had to wage against Charles of Lorraine and a very dangerous opposition.

The study of governmental methods reflects this contradiction. One notices signs of an aggravated decline, a new stage of collapse. But one also observes an apparent desire of the rulers to maintain themselves on the scale of the monarchy of the last Carolingians [and] not without at least temporary success.

This new stage of decline stands out all the more in that it appears, in certain respects, as something definitive. Positions were lost in 987 which would not be regained, at least not before the twelfth century, and [then] in a different way through the action of revived institutions. It is in the perspective of more than a century, the century of the first Capetians (987-1108) that one must locate the characteristics of decadence, which, as they receded, left an imprint that itself underscores the image we may have of the event of 987.

The first [characteristic], one could say, is of a geographic nature. The map of the areas receiving royal documents no longer has the same contours and no longer covers the same areas as in the time of the last Carolingians. Less and less diluted, it reveals larger areas of [royal] absence, with a consistency that defies the hazards of [the] survival [of documents]. This is particularly clear for the southern regions. With exceptions of negligible proportions (less than one hundredth of the total) ... all the land of Languedoc escaped the action of the king ... This absence is particularly suggestive for Gothia and the Spanish March[1] which ... had been liberally endowed with charters by the kings of the old dynasty. After 987 it is finished, totally, abruptly finished, to the point where the break with former usage cannot be explained by any cause other than the political change, by the defiance [now felt] toward a dynasty no longer blessed with legitimacy [and] no longer inspiring the sentiments of loyalty which still sustained the descendants of Charlemagne despite their growing feebleness ... A century after 987, the pope had replaced the king in the vassal fealty of the leaders of this region. This change of dependence may be traced ultimately to the royal weakness of the period of Hugh Capet ...

In addition, from the time of Hugh Capet the weakness of the king induced other powers to exercise certain prerogatives that had formerly been his. And what was more specifically royal in Carolingian times than enforcing the peace, *pax et justitia,* preventing brigandage, and combatting the robbers whom the capitularies of Charlemagne had so often threatened with their sanctions? It is now the episcopate which, independently of the king, instituted the Peace of God. The movement emerged from Aquitaine (Charroux, 989), and from Septimania (Norbonne,

990), before spreading elsewhere.² These places, these dates, underscore one synchronism, one cause—the royal withdrawal.

This absenteeism had its counterpart at the king's court, where the southern princes no longer, or nearly no longer, came. Among the *proceres,* vassals of the king whose signatures at the bottom of royal diplomas certify their presence there, not once, between 987 and 1108 [do the names of] the duke of Gascony, the count of Toulouse, the duke of Gothia, nor the other princes of this region [appear] ... The duke of Aquitaine appeared rarely, on the greatest occasions; the count of Auvergne and the count of LaMarch, under exceptional circumstances. And these were the only ones from south of the Loire ...

The other aspect of decadence concerns the very nature of the royal diploma, which changes. Up to 987, these royal charters were uniformly the object of a subscription by the chancery, joined to a royal subscription and the affixing of royal seals of validation, which gave these documents the validity of public acts whose sole basis was royal authority. After this date, things changed; the king had his charters, or at least some of them, no longer subscribed by the chancellor alone but by the persons with him at the time they were dispatched, a practice influenced by the private charters that were undersigned in this way. [This is] an indication that royal authority was no longer sufficient to back up the decision that the diploma expressed or to guarantee its validity.

The first document undersigned in this way was in the first months of 988, coinciding with the change of dynasty, which well establishes the relation of cause to effect ... A new method of government or, rather, a sign of impotence? An impotence that was going to be prolonged [and] aggravated, [with] the subscriptions becoming a mark of the decline, a means of measuring the collapse. For more than a century they were going to impose themselves in some way on the royal chancery practice, until the end of Philip I's reign. And their rarefaction at that moment and still more under Louis VI would accompany a new recovery of royal authority ...

After 1007-1008, the new methods ... showed a progress to which the following totals testify: whereas under Hugh Capet the acts of the new type (royal diplomas of multiple subscriptions and nonroyal charters undersigned by the king) were still only in a proportion of 1:6 in relation to diplomas of the Carolingian type, and the total remained visibly the same for the first ten years of Robert II's reign [996-1031]. It then rose to the point where it was one-third ... of the total royal acts for the whole period 996-1025 ... That no less underscores the fact that two thirds did not deviate—a sign of the play of forces moderating the evolution.

The social position of the witnesses to the royal charters testifies to the same ... evolution, bounded by the same dates. It started off high, with a royal entourage that absorbed the aristocracy of those holding *honores* and in which the episcopate predominated. Three archbishops and six bishops as compared to one count and his three sons [appearing] at the bottom of a diploma of Hugh Capet in 988 suggested political designs [that were aimed at] prolonging those of Hincmar and the Carolingians of the last century. Besides, had Adalbero of Reims, one of the archbishops, permitted the election of Hugh Capet to the throne the year before with any other intention?[3]

During the first thirty years of the reign of Robert the Pious, up to around 1025-1028, it [was] pretty nearly the same thing, although with certain variations—indications of a slight weakening. The high aristocracy no longer monopolized the entourage of the witnesses. But it still dominated it to the point of obscuring the others . . . 87 out of 105 . . . The [other] 18 were viscounts, castellans, [and] several knights. [Was this an] advance warning of a new decline? Perhaps, but for the moment [it was] still negligible.

Among the seventy-nine witnesses who came from the high aristocracy holding honors, only eighteen were laymen, of which there were only five who came from principalities other than *Francia:* a feeble total that illustrates the progressive narrowing of royal action, the true constant of the history of the tenth and eleventh centuries . . .

The high ecclesiastical and lay aristocracy that surrounded the king and undersigned his documents was restricted to a network of families whose successes often went back to Carolingian times. It was the group of royal *fideles* whose rank was no longer social but juridical, yet tied to the former and like it, prolonging something Carolingian with all the traces of an orderly evolution. Under Hugh Capet, for those who undersigned, there was still no question of intervening in any other capacity . . .

The effort made by the first Capetian generation to maintain a royalty aligned with the last Carolingian century ran aground about the years 1025-1030. This defeat contributed to the decrepitude of a system that collapsed of its own weight because it was moribund. The decline it was going to entail did not affect the methods of government alone; it extended to the collective structures of the society which were injured both by the contraction of the political and social sphere and by a decline in the social scale of the leaders. All this reflected a state of things rather well characterized by what Marc Bloch called "the first feudal age"; it was truly the weaknesses of this age that . . . were reflected and totalized in the royal establishment of the half century [after 1025]. Then, after about 1077, there would be still further prolongations of the decline of preceding times; but, in a new economic environment and also under the impact of quite different political ideas, there would already be signs of recovery. In the fifty years we are dealing with, French kingship was, if the image is permitted, in the trough between the waves, and nothing yet, or nearly nothing, allowed the next revival to be foreseen.

The new degree of collapse that we observe around 1025 took place rather suddenly. And the corner was turned, and turned sharply, in the last years of the reign of Robert the Pious (1025/1028-1031), in the direction in which things were going to progress next under Henry I and the beginning of the reign of Philip I, following a course which scarcely deviated (1031-1077).

The decline is observable from various points of view in the categories of diplomas, from the social and juridical rank of the witnesses, and from the kinds of meetings at which the majority [of diplomas] were witnessed. It created an uneasiness shown by contemporaries, from which grew a sense of decline, nourished by bitterness and deception.

After 1025, the new chancery methods experienced a sharp expansion; the proportion of diplomas of multiple subscriptions, if we join them to the nonroyal charters undersigned by the king, increased in relation to the acts drawn up according to former methods. The two categories were now equal, 13 to 13.

This was, perhaps, keeping in step with the social standing of the witnesses, whose rank dropped. It was after 1028 that the matter was clearer. A half dozen bishops and counts of *Francia,* [along with] the counts of Flanders and Poitou, figured prominently that year, as they had previously, at the bottom of a charter of Robert II, but they were far from being the only ones. Twelve or thirteen castellans or viscounts from the regions of royal influence overshadowed them slightly . . . [In addition there were] six knights. What was new was not the presence of this one or that one . . . [but] their number, or, one could say, their mass; it is that they were grouped together, the lords of the Ile-de-FraNce and the region around Chartres . . .

The bishops and counts submitted to the development. Their former preponderance was weakened. They were obliged to mingle their subscriptions with those of castellans and even of knights [who were] perhaps the fine flower of the French aristocracy—and certain of the castellans at least were very well connected—but a middling or even low aristocracy which put them [the bishops and counts] in a dangerous minority. . . .

Only geography could [have brought] those [diverse] men together and explain their presence. It was the powerful men of a region, no longer the *fideles* of the king, who assembled around him to witness his charters. A considerable difference, which had for its direct cause the descent of the royal entourage on the social scale and, by consequence, an alteration in the very notion of royal government. In gathering his *fideles* for such [occasions] and in only having them witness in this capacity, the king still maintained the fiction of a sort of common summons [as reason] to assemble them from all regions of the kingdom. And it mattered little where they actually came from; the only thing that counted in their presence was, at least in theory, the personal tie that united them to the king. To have called the non-*fideles* only for the reason that politically they dominated such and such a region, was perhaps for the king simply to demonstrate realism. But it was also to admit what the territorial dislocation had now imposed on him, and that he could not—for the moment at least—resist the current that fragmented the kingdom into sectors of domination. It was also to recognize that to figure at the bottom of a royal charter, what mattered was not so much a tie of a feudal nature but power over land—where the territorial restrictions of the 1030s found a new significance and a new expression. Georges Duby has said of this period that it was "less the time of the fiefs than the time of the castles."[4]

Notes

1. The March of Spain was that part of Charlemagne's empire lying south of the Pyrenees, consisting mainly of Catalonia, the region around Barcelona. This territory was nominally part of France until 1258, but it was absorbed into the Spanish political system at least two centuries earlier. Gothia, lying on the northeastern border of the Spanish March, shared the latter's substantial Gothic population, from which it gained its name, but it remained part of southern France (Languedoc) and became subject to the authority of the count of Toulouse in the eleventh century. [Ed.]

2. *Pax et justitia* (peace and justice) were traditional principles of kingship which were taken over by the higher clergy of southern France when they launched the famous Peace of God movement at the end of the tenth century [Ed.].

3. Hincmar, archbishop of Reims (845-882) had argued that kings should act in accordance with the advice of the prelates of the Church. He so enhanced the political importance of the see of Reims that its archbishop often had the decisive voice in who should be king. Thus Archbishop Adalbero had played a vital role in Hugh Capet's election [Ed.].

4. Georges Duby, *La societé aux* XIe et XIIe siécles dans la région mâconnaise (Paris, 1953), p. 364.

Chapter 4 A FEUDAL LORD ON THE THRONE

JOSEPH CALMETTE (1873-1952) was one of France's most prolific writers on medieval history. His works ranged from scholarly articles on early medieval Aquitaine to popular syntheses of important periods and reigns. His works of popular history are notable for a strongly nationalistic tone. This selection is taken from one of these popularizations, dealing with the French monarchy in the period 850-1150. It will be seen that Calmette presents a view of Hugh Capet's accession that is rather different from that of Lemarignier.

The illustrious historian Achille Luchaire very pertinently said that the election of 987 was above all an ecclesiastical act. It was not so solely by reason of the role that the leaders of the church of Reims played in the affair; it was so for more profound reasons, too.

At a moment when . . . the magnates all took for themselves maximum independence, the idea that the throne might be left without an occupant occurred to no one; but the necessity of a king was imposed on no subject of the *regnum Franciae* with as imperious a force as on the men of the Church. For them, the consecration differentiated the *Rex* from all [other] possessors of authority, so great was its

Excerpt from Joseph Calmette, *Le Réveil Capétien*, Librairie Hachette, Editeur, Paris, 1948, pp. 68-72. Reprinted by permission of Librairie Hachette. Translated by John B. Henneman and Thomas R. Prest.

power. Though he [presently] had no effective power, the king consecrated by God was an essential element of the political and social armor of the Christian state.

Thus, in spite of the weakness that the last representatives of the house of Charlemagne, in decline for more than a century and a half, left to their successors, the traditional royalty was theoretically unscathed. On the level of pure ideas, the dynastic duel modified nothing in the essence of sovereignty. Robertian kingship had not differed, in the past, from that of Charles the Bald, Charles the Simple, Louis the Exile. Capetian kingship did not distinguish itself from that of Louis V, either in the minds of the electors or in the mind of the elected.

Is this to say, then, that the substitution of the "third race" for the second affects only nomenclature and that it was henceforth, historically, undifferentiated? It would be a major error to derive such a conclusion from the facts. [Hugh] Capet, in whose veins no Carolingian blood flowed, carried to the throne the mentality of a *dux* [duke]. He remained a duke in becoming king. The legend that encircles one of his coins points up ... this significant aspect of the crucial hour; [it is] a legend that curiously mingles the two terms and is formulated thus: *Hugo dux gratia Dei rex*.[1]

What should one deduce from this remarkable avowal? King in the Carolingian manner, on the level of ideas, Capet acted, in the daily reality of concrete facts, as a duke, that is to say, feudally. He did not struggle, as did the Carolingians, to save at all cost the greatest possible amount of the sovereign power of the golden age ... The Capetian, to tell the truth, did not possess a very precise notion of this sovereign power in his feudal capacity.

With him was realized, therefore, what no Carolingian ever wanted to accept—in him royalty identified in practice with suzerainty. The Capetian king would be the king of the Church, certainly; but he would be the suzerain of the feudal territories.

To believe that the man elected in 987 owed the votes to his feudal position is certainly an error. He was seen no more as the champion of feudalism than as the champion of the elective right. He was chosen because, besides himself, only Charles of Lorraine could aspire to the throne and Charles was not wanted. But it remains that Capet, although king, was and remained what he had previously been, a feudal lord ...

Capetian kingship, indelibly marked with the unction of the consecration, kept its original virtue intact. [But it] had to dissimulate it for a long time under formulas [that were] purely decorative in appearance and to absorb it into a task that seems, at first glance, only to have the character of a moral mission.

On the other hand, whereas the Carolingian, king to the bottom of his heart, did not act as suzerain except when constrained and forced as a last resort, it will be seen that on the contrary the duke-king and his successors after him displayed openly, and with a visible complaisance, after, as well as before, the turning point of 987, their suzerain prerogatives. They assumed the feudal aspect without a backward glance and without discomfort, and it is in this change of the psychology of the chief that the substitution of "race" finds its true import.

As a feudal king, the Capetian would reconcile the law of the crown to that of the fief. He put himself in this situation to which no Carolingian [would] condescend. To complete the account, how, without aid, did the Church, in crowning Capet in 987, save the crown? An unconscious disguise covers the unperceived equivocation. The prince that calls himself *dux* and *rex* at the same time is not perceptive enough to discern the antinomy of the two terms that he juxtaposes. His myopia is a miraculous guarantee that he shall accomplish without hindrance the exceptionally fruitful mission that destiny reserved to him.

The Capet king has the honor; but perhaps it will be more to his grief.

The election that was decided at Compiégne took place officially at Noyon, and the coronation followed on 3 July, 987. [And there was] already opposition [by] Archbishop Seguin of Sens, count Albert of Vermandois and perhaps also of the Flemings. The new king triumphed easily enough over these first obstacles. He felt ... assured enough to promise to count Borel of Barcelona, who solicited his aid against the Saracens, [that he would] place himself at the head of the French chivalry in order to drive the enemies outside the Catalan borders.

Was he, however, so sure of himself that he thought seriously of crossing the Pyrenees? What [are we] to think of a program of such scope? The naiveté of an optimist or the astuteness of a well-advised realist? Still, the appeal did come from across the mountains and the project of an expedition to Spain served as a pretext for the assembly at Orléans. The magnates who were assembled there saw the plan of campaign set forth, [saw] the necessity that in the absence of the sovereign a substitute [should] take his place, [and saw] the opportunity to consecrate the royal prince Robert. In conclusion—would this be the key to the whole scenario?—Robert, on Christmas day 987, was crowned and associated with the paternal authority. Henceforth, [it was spoken] currently and conjointly of the *kings* Hugh and Robert. The skillful maneuver that assured the continued existence of the young dynasty had fully succeeded. Robert, student of Gerbert,[2] was the son of that Adelaide of Aquitaine in whom the Carolingian blood was revived.

Notes

1. "Duke Hugh, by the Grace of God, King." [Ed.].

2. Gerbert of Aurillac, who later became Pope Sylvester II (999-1003) was the most renowned teacher and scholar of the late tenth century [Ed.].

Part Three
REVIVAL OF KINGSHIP UNDER THE CAPETIANS

Chapter 5 THE CAPETIAN MIRACLE OF HEALING

MARC BLOCH (1886-1944) is sometimes called the greatest French medievalist of the twentieth century. Best known to American students for his *Feudal Society,* he has had a great influence on French historiography. Bloch criticized the narrow focus of institutional historians and those who treated history as the achievements of a few great men. He called for a new history that would employ a wide variety of previously untapped sources in order to describe the way of life and the psychology of the mass of ordinary people. The present excerpts are but a fragment of his long work on thaumaturgical kingship, the belief in royal healing powers.

Our ancestors in the Middle Ages and in more recent times had a picture of royalty very different from our own. In those days every country considered kings as sacred persons, and in some countries at least they were held to possess miraculous powers of healing. For many centuries, the kings of France and the kings of England used to "touch for scrofula," to use the classical expression of the time. That is to say, they claimed to be able, simply by their touch, to cure people suffering from this disease, and there was common belief in their medicinal powers among their subjects. Over an almost equally long period, the kings of England used to distribute to

From the forthcoming English edition of Marc Bloch, *The Royal Touch* (London and Montreal, 1972), originally published in French as *Les Rois thaumaturges* (Paris, 1924). Printed by permission of Routledge and Kegan Paul Ltd., McGill-Queen's University Press, and Librairie Armand Colin. This selection corresponds to parts of the following pages of the original French edition: 17-18, 27-28, 40, 60-61, 68-70, and 79-82.

their subjects, and even beyond the boundaries of their own State, the so-called cramp rings which, by virtue of their consecration at the hands of the king, were held to have acquired the power to restore health to the epileptic, and assuage all kinds of muscular pain. These facts are well known to the learned and to those who are interested in such matters. Yet it must be admitted that they are peculiarly repugnant to the modern mind, and are therefore usually passed over in silence. Historians have written massive books on the idea of royalty without ever mentioning them . . .

The ganglia most easily attacked by tuberculosis are those of the neck; and when the disease goes untreated, and suppurations occur, the face may easily appear to be affected. Hence a confusion, apparent in many of the documents, between scrofula and various other afflictions of the face or even the eyes. Tubercular adenitis is very widespread, even nowadays; so what must it have been like in conditions of hygiene notably inferior to our own? If we mentally add the other kinds of adenitis, and all the vague group of miscellaneous diseases popularly confused with them, we shall have some idea of the ravages attributable to what Europe of old used to include under the name of "scrofula." In certain regions, as both medieval and modern doctors testify, these diseases were virtually endemic. This is hardly ever a fatal disease; but especially where there is a failure to give the appropriate treatment, it is very trying and disfiguring . . . The background picture, then, which the historian of the royal miracle should keep in mind, is that of countless sufferers longing for healing, and ready to have recourse to any remedies popularly held in common esteem.

I have already reminded the reader of what this miracle was. In France of old it was called "le mal de roi"; in England, the King's Evil. The kings of France and of England claimed that a simple touch with their hands, made according to the traditional rites, was able to cure the scrofulous. When did they begin to exercise this miraculous power? How were they led to make this claim? And how did their subjects come to recognize it? . . .

We can feel sure we are on solid ground if we sum up as follows: Robert the Pious, the second Capetian, was held by his faithful admirers to possess the gift of healing the sick. His successors inherited his power; but as it passed down the generations, this dynastic virtue became gradually modified or rather grew more precise. The idea arose that the royal touch was a sovereign remedy, not for all diseases indiscriminantly, but in particular for one extremely widespread disease, scrofula; and by the time of Philip I, Robert's grandson, this transformation had been accomplished . . .

The revolution in religion did, indeed, strike a redoubtable blow at the ancient concept of sacred royalty as it flourished among the Teutons. Through the advent of Christianity it was stripped of its natural support, the national paganism. The kings continued to exist as heads of state, and for a short while after the invasions their political power was even stronger than ever before; but they ceased, at least officially, to be considered divine persons. No doubt the old ideas did not die out all at once. They probably continued to live on more or less obscurely in the popular consciousness. Our documents show traces of this now and again, and we should probably discover many more if our sources were not all ecclesiastical in origin, and as a result hostile to the past on this particular point. The long hair constituting the traditional attribute of the Frankish dynasty (all other freemen wore their hair short as soon as they were adult) had certainly been at the beginning a symbol of something supernatural . . .

It was never by virtue of their kingship that the Merovingians received unction; and this applies, as we need hardly remind ourselves, to Clovis, no less than to the others . . .Legend much later in the day converted the ceremony carried out by St. Rémi at Rheims into the first royal consecration, though it was in truth no more than a simple baptism. But in 751 Pepin, boldly risking the step his father Charles Martel had not dared to take, decided to consign to a convent the last descendants of Clovis, and to claim royal honours as well as royal power. He then felt the need to colour his usurpation with a sort of religious presitige. There is no doubt that the kings of old had always been considered by their faithful supporters far superior to the rest of the people; but the vague aura of mysticism surrounding them was solely due to the influence upon the collective consciousness of obscure memories dating from pagan times. The new dynasty, on the other hand, possessing an authentic sacrosanctity, were to owe their consecration to a definite act justified by the Bible and fully Christian . . . .Thus Pepin became the first of the French kings to receive unction from the hands of priests, after the manner of the Hebrew chiefs. "It is manifest to all men," he announced proudly in one of his proclamations, "that Divine Providence has raised us by anointing to this throne." His successors were not slow to follow his example . . .

At the same time a second rite with a different origin was being joined on to it. On 25 December 800, in the basilica of St. Peter, Pope Leo III had placed a "crown" on the head of Charlemagne, and proclaimed him emperor. This was no doubt a golden circle, like the one that had for many centuries replaced the diadem . . . For the first time at Rheims in 816, his son, Louis the Pious, received from Pope Stephen IV, along with the imperial title, the anointing with holy oil as well as the crown. From that time onwards, the two actions became more or less inseparable . . .

The first French sovereign thought to have healed the sick was Robert the Pious. Now Robert was the second representative of a new dynasty. He received the royal title and anointing in his father Hugh's lifetime, as early as 987, that is to say, in the very year of the usurpation. The Capetians were successful, and that is why it is not easy to imagine how frail their power must have seemed in those early years. Yet we know that it was in fact contested. There was great prestige attached to the Carolingians, and since 936 no one had dared to dispute their right to the crown. It needed a hunting accident (causing the death of Louis V) and an international intrigue to make their fall a possibility. In 987, and even later, who could have been certain that they had fallen for good? For many, no doubt, this association of father and son on the throne was only an interim measure: as Gerbert wrote in 989 or 990, they were only "kings provisionally" (*interreges*). For a long time there were centres of opposition, notably at Sens, and in the South . . . In short, the most urgent task confronting the Capetians was to reestablish the legitimacy of their line to their own advantage . . . In very similar conditions, the Carolingians had fallen back upon a biblical rite, royal unction. It is surely very possible for the appearance of the healing power under Robert II to be explained as the result of the same kind of solicitude as had formerly prompted Pepin to imitate the example of the Hebrew princes. To affirm this would be presumptuous; but it is certainly a tempting supposition.

Of course, it was not simply a matter of cold calculation. Robert enjoyed a great reputation for personal piety, which probably explains why the Capetian miracle began with him and not with his father Hugh. The saintly character attributed to the king as a human being, together with the sanctity inherent in royalty, must quite naturally have led his subjects to credit him with wonder-working gifts of healing. We can if we like suppose that the first people who asked for the royal touch at a date we are never likely to know did so of their own accord . . .

Up to, at the earliest, the year 1100, Robert II and his descendants were the only European kings to touch for scrofula; the other kings, although "the Lord's anointed," did not attempt to heal. It would seem then that something else besides unction was needed to convey this wonderful talent. To make a real king, a really sainted king, something else was required beyond an election followed by consecration: ancestral virtue was still an element that counted for something. The persistence of the claims to miraculous healing powers in the Capetian line certainly did not by itself create that faith in the legitimacy of their family which was to prove one of the best supports of the French crown. Precisely the opposite was the case: the idea of this inherited miracle was only accepted because there still lingered on in men's hearts some trace of the ancient notions concerning hereditarily sacred families. Yet it cannot be doubted that the spectacle of these royal healings served to strengthen this feeling and somehow renew its youth. The second Capetian had begun the marvel; his descendants, much to the benefit of the monarchy, made it no longer the prerogative of a particular king, but of the whole dynasty . . .

Chapter 6 SIGNS OF REVIVAL AFTER 1077

Continuing his study of the early Capetian monarchy and government, JEAN-FRANCOIS LEMARIGNIER introduces a subject that he has studied in a number of other scholarly works—the spread of federated reformed monasticism and the Gregorian reform in the Church. At first opposed to the march of the monastic federations, the crown found itself unable to resist the powerful religious currents of the eleventh century. Lemarignier suggests that in the end the reform movement had an important impact on the French monarchy, one that differed from its impact in other countries.

One of the most delicate problems posed by the western revival of the eleventh and twelfth centuries is how to know at what time to date its origin. Marc Bloch proposed to place the break around the middle of the eleventh century. Very evidently, without fixing it at a single moment, it is proper to join this very great historian in choosing that time, since it marked the most acknowledged turning point and witnessed the decisive options that were going to lead from the first feudal age to the second. However, the change that was effected was of such magnitude that it was not realized exactly at the same time from all the points of view involved nor in all the regions or levels of society that it affected. To consider French kingship, we cannot truly speak of recovery until after 1108, under the

From Jean-François Lemarignier, *Le gouvernement royal aux premiers temps capétiens (987-1108)* (Paris, 1965), pp. 141-150, 153, 157-160, 167-171, 176. Reprinted by permission of A. et J. Picard et Cie. Translated by John B. Henneman and Rosalie A. Vermette.

reign of Louis VI. But certain of the traits which were going to mark his ascendancy were already discernible in the last thirty years of the reign of Philip I, permitting a presage of the revival that would lead to it.

An impression of revival arose already from a concentration of religious establishments which, if it involved the crown only obliquely, was not on that account foreign to its action or ignored in its diplomas. There was something rather new here, one could say rather sudden, but [there] was also an indication of a reversal of conditions. The multiplication of sanctuaries which, in the first three-quarters of the eleventh century, had been one of the essential aspects of the religious transformation of the Ile-de-France, had contributed in no small way to rendering more vivid the color of the anarchy with which this region was tinted. And the image was rendered more impressive by contrast with the neighboring regions where order in the regular church had been created or recreated by the action of cohesive, even confederating, monasticism. So [it was] in the North of the kingdom and also in Lorraine through the action of Richard of Saint-Vanne and under the form of personal union and unity of observance. [It happened] in the same way in Normandy, thanks to William of Volpiano and the political intelligence of the dukes, while in northern Burgundy the same William had stimulated a movement and created centers of monastic life which were not without connections with the Norman centers. In the South, Cluny progressively federated Aquitaine; in the West, in the regions of Maine, Dunois, and Vendomois, Marmoutier had successfully undertaken this federative work . . . In the midst of these [monastic] collectives, the regions of royal influence in the years around 1077 seemed like an islet of anarchical predominance [where there was], up to a certain point, an incidence of religious structures more disassociated from political structures than elsewhere.

Efforts at reconstruction were going to converge on this islet from the neighboring regions of cohesion, through the process of regrouping. The first mark of the revival that was going to expand after 1077 was its external source. The second was its monastic origin; the collegiate churches, which were perhaps the establishments that had the most to gain, had only been interested in establishing themselves in a monastic federation by means of priories, sometimes only for awhile. In the years around 1077 only the great monasteries had the resources needed to unite, federate, and expand. At the sources of this convergence, three monasteries, or groups of monasteries from the neighboring regions, played a predominant role. There was, in the first place, the Norman group. Several Norman abbeys penetrated into the Ile-de-France . . . Parallel to the Norman push was that of Marmoutier . . . [But] in this monastic regrouping it was Cluny that finally had the greatest success, not only by the renown of the federating monastery but also by that of the collegiate church federated, none other than Saint-Martin-des-Champs.[2] The Cluniac monks, having decided around 1077 to cross the Loire, which up to then had marked one of the limits of their progress, established themselves . . . at Lewes in England in 1077 and two years later at the Parisian collegiate church, which they made into a priory . . .

Philip I, forced to renounce the policy of independence *vis-à-vis* the papacy attempted by Henry I, recognized implicitly that it was impossible for him to resist the Gregorians; and he admitted that the French crown would abandon definitively the old Carolingian positions to which Henry I had been desperately clinging, and [Philip] outlined the new orientation that was to lead him into the wake of the Roman Church.

The king was not alone in being involved in these affiliations that transformed the religious structures of the regions under their influence. His entourage was equally [involved] ... It remains evident that the aristocracy of the Ile-de-France took its part in the monastic affiliations, which could only increase their impact.

The new traits, which after 1077 were going to modify the aspect of the royal entourage and more generally testify to changes in the methods of government, were not all to be recorded on the side of recovery. There were some things that merely prolonged the earlier decline, such as the increase of witnessing in connection with the diplomas, or increased proliferation of lesser people, which we need not discuss further. There were otherthings that pertained to causes foreign to kingship ... [such as] the revival of the economy, which ... explains the subscription of several bourgeois after 1080.

It is equally in the realm of circumstances outside the king's action that we must place the desertion of the high aristocracy from the ranks of those witnessing royal charters. [The] retirement [of the high aristocracy] is particularly evident with respect to the episcopate. The rise of the knights and castellans in the royal entourage in the years after 1028 had not, on this account, discouraged the diligence of the bishops. The latter still came to the king's court in relatively large numbers; and if the geographic area of their dependencies had receded, their density and cohesion had only declined a little. From 1060 to 1077, their subscriptions were maintained at one-fifth of the total, 129 out of 675. This implied assemblies—there were seven or eight of them—in which there were around ten [bishops] with the king, constituting the predominant element of the court that he had formed for a day ... After [1077] it is no longer thus. Rather abruptly the bishops no longer, or nearly no longer, come ... From 1077 to 1108, their subscriptions fall from one-fifth to one-thirteenth of the total ...

The change seems to have been due in part to the influence of the Gregorian reform. The year 1077, in which [the bishops] stopped [attending court], was also that in which the legate Hugh of Die imposed the rigor of his methods on a restive episcopate. At the council of Autun ... in September, he convoked archbishops and bishops, and judged and condemned them. He struck at the simoniacs[3] ... All these prelates were royal prelates, assiduous at the king's court and the witnesses of his charters. But Philip I was powerless to defend them against the sanctions of Hugh of Die. Belittled, deceived, forced to be present at synods of the legates ... the bishops deserted the royal entourage ...

The flight of the bishops from the royal entourage was accompanied by that of the counts, which was completely proportional. From 1060 to 1077 their subscriptions were still one-eighth of the total (84 of 675). They fell to one-twenty-fifth (18 out of 460), that is, by two-thirds. Bishops and counts no longer surrounded the witnesses of middling rank, whose social standing, moreover, continued to decline. The instability also [increased], for the more their social rank diminished, the more often these [persons] changed from one occasion to another, and these [changes] became very frequent. This evolution would have led to an aggravated anarchy but for the rise of a new category, the great officers of the king, whose progress amounted to a first and essential aspect of the recovery that was taking form in these [last] thirty years [of Philip I's reign].

The great officers of the king, that is to say, in this period, the seneschal, constable, chamberlain, and butler, appeared in the time of Henry I [r. 1031-1060], and it was in 1043 that two of them, the constable and butler, undersigned a royal diploma for the first time ... The subscriptions of the great officers were, from the time of Henry I, rather numerous ... The great officers became increasingly involved. Two undersigned together in 1043; then, for the first time, three in 1048; and four in 1059-1060. This process was amplified under Philip I. From 1060 to 1077, out of forty-six charters with multiple subscriptions, thirty-three carried those of the great officers, or around two-thirds; and sixteen were witnessed by the four acting as a group and forming a corporate body. The percentage of their subscriptions, still only one-fourteenth of the total under Henry I (22 of 313) rose to more than one-seventh (102 of 675).

From 1077 to 1108, the proportions would be even greater ... reaching one-fifth (85 of 460). And then certain new facts also had great importance, in themselves and by their continuation. In 1084, for the first time, a charter was witnessed only by the four great officers. This action was repeated in 1091 and again in 1104, 1106, and 1107 ...

In the last years of the reign of Philip I, the usage was well established, favored by the king, and sanctioned by the charters that the great officers dominated his palace, coordinated his entourage, and led the witnesses of his acts. The advantage that the crown was able to derive from their rise would not have been possible if, on the one hand, it had not been progressive ... and, on the other, it had not been adaptable to social conditions. The great officers constituted the new political team, but they were drawn from families who, much earlier, had acquired preponderance around the king ... They belonged to the world of the castellans of the Ile-de-France, older or younger branches, greater or lesser castellans, and also [of the] knights. One finds among them differences of power or fortune and multiple nuances that separated some from others, but [there were] also ties of blood that united them and enabled them collectively to form a veritable aristocracy of the Ile-de-France ...

What is certain is that finally the king knew how to draw some men, whose stability paved the way for the later revival, from an entourage which had not ceased to decline in social rank and cohesiveness.... and [their emergence] was a sign of recovery in the last thirty years of the reign of Philip I.

A sign nearly as certain was the rise of the royal provosts, although at a less elevated level of what one could call the administration: no longer central, but local (if these words do not convey some anachronism). [The provosts] appeared in 1057 among the witnesses of Henry I's charters; then they intervened in three sessions, one after the other, in the last years of the reign of that prince. Under Philip I, [the occasions of] their presence amplified at first; increasing, up to 1082, at a rate roughly proportional to that we have just noted for the great officers...

After 1082, the charters of Philip I offer only rare subscriptions by the provosts [who only witnessed] acts, moreover, in which no great officers participated. Their rather sudden retirement, which extended to more than half his reign, contrasts with the growing presence of the great officers... It could well be connected with a change in the methods of royal government and the appearance of writs (*mandements*). The writ was an order of the king, and [Achille] Luchaire could write that "it is to the provosts that the royal writs are formally addressed." One of the diplomas between 1082 and 1108 witnessed by the provosts is a short order of the king prohibiting the provost of Paris from levying exactions on the men of Bagneux and conscripting them into the army. By its form, object, and addressee, it has the look of a writ. Should the apparent flight of the provosts from the royal entourage then be explained by the rise of the writ, which was, beyond a doubt, another sign of recovery?

The writ was an order of the king. It was expressed in the concise form of a letter that ... did not carry any subscriptions [by witnesses]. These external characteristics that made the writ different from the diploma lead one to equate the writs to simple royal letters, ... They expressed the tone of command, as the king ordered, or else forbade some action ... These features bear witness to a strengthening of royal authority. No Capetian diploma, going back to 987, had procured anything other than a title to the exercise of a right, and it was up to him who received it to take advantage of it and obtain what it granted...

The royal recovery, which was hinted at under Philip I, became evident under Louis VI. Less uncertain, less fragmentary, it no longer was limited to a few changes in the methods of government and to progress in the exercise of justice; it was translated into political successes. The king became the master of the Ile-de-France. He extended his action further in the kingdom, and from Flanders to Auvergne his efforts were not without success. Of the facts which characterized or clarified the strengthening of his authority, we shall confine ourselves to only two types: those which prolonged the recovery outlined in the reign of Philip I, [and] those which contrasted with the weaknesses of the preceding century.

The first will be the object of only brief observations. That the writs must have been expanded appears probable, although "their tradition has not been favorable," and only a small number are known to us. But from the use that Louis VI made of them in the Flemish affair of 1127-1128,[4] it is clear that they had been a means of government for the king and doubtless a normal means. The progress of the great officers in the royal entourage involves less of a hypothesis. [Let us] consider thirty-three of Louis VI's diplomas of multiple subscriptions concerning Paris: twenty, that is more than half, were witnessed only by the great officers; eight, by them and other witnesses. The tendency to eliminate the witnesses is already very evident; it prevailed definitively under Louis VII. The progressive reduction of the subscriptions coincided with a recovery of royal authority, just as their increase after Hugh Capet was connected to its decline . . .

The strengthening of the king's justice was another sign of the rise of his authority, prolonging the successes of Prince Louis in the last years of the reign of Philip I. Better than a mere indication, it carried the direct mark [of growing authority] with consequences that Suger[5] has preserved in order to better establish the image of kingship on the march. The geography of royal interventions became enlarged. And from the beginning of his reign, Louis VI did not hesitate to affirm his judicial power well outside the progressively restricted circle in which his Capetian predecessors had confined their action, especially farther south . . .

The strengthened justice of the king was not without a connection, notably in the eyes of Suger, to the idea of suzerainty, to the principle of a feudal hierarchy working to the king's benefit. To conclude, we touch here upon a question that will be the final hypothesis of the research on which this work is based. Did there exist, in the eleventh century, a pyramidal hierarchy, or, again to take up the definition of the old feudalists, a double correlation of persons and lands from step to step culminating at the summit with the kingdom and the king? Or else, on the contrary, was not this notion, which was so much to sustain the buildup of monarchical authority after Louis VI and Suger, something new in contrast to the feudal anarchy of the preceding century?

The royal diplomas of the eleventh century do not reveal, in the minds of those who wrote them or who lived in the ambiance of which they were the expression, any idea of hierarchy in the sense we have just set forth. The society whose image they reflect was molded, at the end of the tenth and the first quarter of the eleventh centuries, by the decomposition of the Carolingian state and by that territorial disassociation that, step by step, placed the political leaders at the level of the *banale* lordship by around the years 1025-1030 . . .

This progressive construction of a doctrine of royal suzerainty and feudal hierarchy taking support from the king was, in the twelfth and thirteenth centuries, to favor the Capetian ascendancy. Suger, exempt abbot of Saint-Denis, who had contributed so much to the building of it, was influenced by Gregorian ideas. "He is like someone from the Roman curia in the presence of the king," wrote Saint Bernard to [Pope] Eugene III. Would he not have sought to have the French monarchy profit from what these ideas could give him concerning the strength of hierarchical authority, which constituted their basis? In which case, the Gregorian reform, whose success finally led to the decline of the German monarchy, would have favored the French monarchy.

Notes

1. Richard of Saint-Vanne and William of Volpiano were eleventh century monastic reformers. Of the various federations of reformed monasteries, the most famous was that headed by the Burgundian abbey of Cluny [Ed.]

2. The collegiate church was organized around a group of clergy called canons, usually presided over by an official called a dean. Saint-Martin-des-Champs was a wealthy royal collegiate church near Paris which became a Cluniac priory in 1079 [Ed.]

3. Pope Gregory VII (1073-1085), sent out legates such as Hugh of Die to root out simoniacs—those who gave or received money in exchange for a church office [Ed.].

4. Louis VI tried to intervene in the disputed succession to the county of Flanders in 1127-1128 [Ed.].

5. Suger (d. 1151) was abbot of Saint-Denis, adviser to Louis VI and Louis VII, and biographer of the former [Ed.].

Chapter 7 LOUIS VI AND THE ENFORCEMENT OF JUSTICE

ACHILLE LUCHAIRE (1846-1908), one of the greatest French medievalists, taught at both Bordeaux and Paris. The author of valuable monographs on the towns and institutions of medieval France and a biography of Pope Innocent III, Luchaire is perhaps best known to American students for his social history of the period of Philip II's reign. The selection here is taken from his lengthy introduction to a work that inventories the documentary and narrative sources dealing with Louis VI.

During the major part of the eleventh century, the reigning family showed itself much more concerned with retaining and exercising the general prerogatives that the Carolingians had enjoyed than [with] assuring their real authority inside their hereditary patrimony. By inertia or by impotence, they let the work of dissolution and usurpation, which was the fatal consequence of the triumph of feudalism, take place all around them with the most extreme results . . .

There rose up everywhere, in the innermost recesses of the Ile-de-France, illegitimate powers, lines of hereditary castellans which were difficult to root out once they had been allowed to grow up. The Capetian soil was covered with hostile *donjons*,[1] permanent obstacles to the security of commerce and even of the great

From Achille Luchaire, *Louis VI le Gros, Annales de sa vie et de son régne* (Paris, 1890), pp. lxv-lxxii. Reprinted by permission of Editions A. et J. Picard et Cie. Translated by John B. Henneman.

cities, and intolerable scourges for the inhabitants of the countryside. The king of France, in spite of the dignity of his title, had reached the point of no longer daring to move about in his own limited domain. He to whom the most powerful lords owed liege homage could not go out of Paris without encountering fortresses built by noble brigands, the terror of merchants, clerics, and peasants. Denuded of money and soldiers, living off its diminished patrimony, the royalty, which had kept a certain measure of prestige outside and in the fiefs at the extremities of the kingdom and in foreign lands, no longer obtained either obedience or respect at home. Enemy territory began two steps from the capital; the great tower of Montlhéry sufficed to make the heir of two Frankish dynasties, the successor of Charlemagne, old with chagrin. One could foresee the moment when the Capetian, no longer possessing the virtual authority attached to the crown, a royal shadow rather than king, would end like the last Carolingian.

The imminence of danger led to a salutary reaction, the effects of which were already becoming manifest before the end of the reign of Philip I. That prince was less incapable and less inert than has been said. At least he had the merit of understanding that to restore monarchical power it was necessary to give it a solid base of support by reconstituting the domain. So he was the first to follow that policy of territorial acquisitions to which Louis the Fat [Louis VI] and Philip Augustus [Philip II] especially were to attach their names. But such work could not be accomplished only by pacific means. To have the reigning dynasty regain its property and its rights, to free the Capetian land from the tyrannies that oppressed it, and to suppress brigandage, negotiations and diplomacy no longer sufficed. War was required, a bitter, pitiless war waged against enemies both numerous and redoubtable through their tenacity and perfidy; a war of bold strokes and furious assaults. [That], in a word, [was what] was required to reduce adversaries solidly entrenched behind the walls of their *donjons*. This military action, continuous and all offensive, was no longer the work for a king like Philip I . . . It happened that the royal prince [Louis VI] was the most energetic and indefatigable of soldiers . . .

Louis applied himself to this rough task as soon as he was invested with the title and powers of king-designate. It is true that from the beginning he presented himself, not as the defender of royal interests charged with reclaiming the rights of the monarchy against usurpation and feudal turbulence, but as the protector of the weak and oppressed and especially as the avenger of the ministers of God, clerks and monks despoiled by the castellans. The Capetian monarchy had always attributed to itself, from the first moment of its institution, this role of sovereign lawgiver and guardian of Church property. But Louis the Fat proclaimed more often and more proudly than anybody, in the preambles of his charters, the need for the kings to defend the beleaguered Church . . . Nearly all the expeditions of Louis the Fat, in effect, were undertaken to give satisfaction to the complaints of a bishop or abbot. The king thus always fought more or less for a holy cause. In offering the help of his sword to those who represented God on earth, he only appeared to be the executor of His will and the instrument of His justice.

We must have respect for the chivalrous sentiments that really inspired Louis and made him the protector of the feeble; but we must also recognize that the interest of the crown almost always coincided with that of the Church. The despoilers of bishops and abbots ordinarily were, at the same time, rebellious vassals in contempt of royal authority. We especially must not forget that the property of the chapters and monasteries in the Île-de-France was in a great part royal property... The bishops and abbots supplemented the insufficiency of domainal revenues. They supplied the army with their soldiers. It was not for them a question of benevolent concession but a duty corresponding to the double right of suzerainty and patronage which the king exercized over his churches; a duty all the more extensive and rigorous when applied to a community nearer to the seat of the monarchy, more immediately dependent on the crown. In defending the lands and revenues of the royal churches against the feudatories, Louis only satisfied the most pressing interests of his own domination and treasury. He fought for his own property.

The task which he set himself was all the more rough in that these tyrants of the Île-de-France more than once succeeded in linking their cause with that of the most redoubtable enemies of the dynasty, the count of Blois, Thibaut IV, and the king of England, Henry I. Let us add that some of them were terrible adversaries, with a singular capacity for evil, able to make a law enforcer less intrepid than the son of Philip I tremble.

The usual misdeeds of these enemies of Church and king are well known. To come to sleep and eat in an abbey or cloister with horses and hunting dogs; to take wine, grain, and livestock from the peasants of the monks; to rob the merchants who went to royal or ecclesiastical fairs—such was their day-to-day existence. But there were some of them who carried out brigandage so scandalously and in such extraordinary proportions that posterity will never be able to forget their names. It is sufficient to cite Hugh of Puiset and Thomas of Marle.

The former was descended from a feudal line that counted among its great deeds the shameful ambush inflicted on Philip I and the imprisonment of [Bishop] Ivo of Chartres. Stationed in the rich plains of the Beauce, like a ravening wolf in the midst of a sheepfold, [Hugh] "devoured," according to the energetic expression of Suger,[2] "all the ecclesiastical lands of the country," and paid no attention to excommunications. When the victims of his depredations assembled at Melun in 1111 to implore royal justice, the count of Chartres, the archbishop of Sens, the abbot of Saint-Denis, the bishop of Chartres, the bishop of Orléans, and the abbots of Fleuri–Saint-Aignan, Saint-Pére-de-Chartres, and Saint-Jean-en-Vallée—appeared among the plaintiffs. But only the powerful dared to complain; the crowd of obscure people who were oppressed resigned themselves to suffering in silence. This brigand was the most crafty, the most untouchable, that one can imagine. Three times the castle of Puiset was besieged, taken, and burned by the royal troops.

Hugh, put under the ban, solemnly dispossessed of his possessions, even imprisoned in the tower of Château-Landon, never admitted defeat. Freed under oath, he wasted no time in rebuilding his *donjon*, making an alliance with the enemies of the king, and resuming his exploits as a malefactor. Suger compared him to a furious dog, whom blows and the chain exasperated and who bit and tore with all the more rage at those whom he had the misfortune to encounter.

Trapped for a last time in 1118 and lost without resources, he had the pleasure, before succumbing, of running through with his lance the seneschal Anseau de Garlande, the favorite of Louis VI whose loss the king long mourned . . .

Hugh of Puiset was only one type of robber baron. Thomas of Marle, a scoundrel on a larger scale, personified the most odious excesses of the feudal regime. He was of that family of Coucy whose arrogant *donjon* still stands, a formidable monument [that] still seems to defy the wrath of heaven and the justice of men, as did those who inhabited it in former times . . . The dominant trait of his character was a refined cruelty which astonished contemporaries in an epoch whose customs were far from gentle. Guibert of Nogent[3] speaks only with terror of the ingenuity that [Thomas] displayed in inventing new tortures and the voluptuous pleasure he took in spilling human blood himself. Here it was not a question of unconscious brutality, which in this period was common to all men of war. Thomas of Marle loved to torment at his leisure those who could not defend themselves, the peasant without weapons or the chained prisoner. "One cannot imagine," adds Guibert, "the number of those whom hunger, torture, and putrefaction have caused to perish in his prisons."

Such a man no more dreaded the warnings of the Church than he did the threats of his father and his neighbors. When the burghers of Laon killed their bishop, an execrable crime in the eyes of contemporaries, Thomas gave asylum to the conspirators. He himself did not hesitate to have his own relative, Gautier, archdeacon of Laon, butchered. One cannot estimate the number of anathemas which were pronounced against him in the courts of the archbishops, bishops, abbots, in the general and provincial councils, in the court of the king. Eventually, he was excommunicated every Sunday in all the parishes of the region. Inaccessible in the depths of his castles, which thick forests protected, for thirty years he defied the impotent efforts of clerics and laymen. In 1114, the papal legate, Conon, bishop of Preneste, had to organize a veritable crusade against the public enemy, with the promise of indulgences or absolution for all those who took part. The direction of the expedition was confided to Louis the Fat, who took the leadership with his usual intrepidness. But the feudal lords showed less enthusiasm; they sent him only insignificant reinforcements. He had to act mainly with the militia of the parishes led by bishops and priests. This time Thomas lost two of his castles and was obliged to indemnify the king and the churches for the damage he had made them suffer.

This was very soft treatment for a criminal so many times excommunicated. Scarcely had the royal army disappeared than he resumed his brigandage. It continued for fifteen more years, proof of the terror he inspired and the impossibility, in the view of the king and the Church, of reducing him by force. Only in 1130 was it decided to do so, when Raoul of Vermandois,[4] a personal enemy of Thomas of Marle, used his influence with Louis the Fat to have organized an expedition which the bishops had urged with entreaties for a long time. This time human justice was satisfied. Pursued into Coucy, mortally wounded and brought to Laon a prisoner, the bandit died as he had lived . . .

Comparable examples show better than any theoretical consideration the necessity of the "clearing away" toward which the king of France was going to work in all parts of his domain, representing the principle of peace and justice. Fighting for his own interests and for the rights of his churches, he performed, at the same time, the work of defending society. Happily for him and for the kingship, he did not always encounter such redoutable adversaries.

Notes

1. A *donjon* was the keep, or fortified tower, that formed the principal defensive feature of the early twelfth century castle [Ed.].

2. See note 5 in the preceding selection for information on Suger [Ed.].

3. Guibert of Nogent was an abbot of the early twelfth century who has left a highly instructive autobiography [Ed.].

4. Raoul, count of Vermandois (d. 1152), was a cousin of the king who held the office of royal seneschal under Louis VII [Ed.].

Chapter 8 FROM GRANDEUR TO PRUDENCE: THE POLICY OF LOUIS VII

MARCEL PACAUT (b. 1920), professor of history at Lyon, has specialized in the study of the three great personalities of continental Europe during the third quarter of the twelfth century: Pope Alexander III, Louis VII of France, and the German emperor Frederick I. The selection printed here is from his book on Louis VII and it goes a long way to rehabilitating that sometimes maligned monarch.

In 1137, neither the political situation nor the condition of the economy and society were pointing in the direction of unity . . . Cohesion, however, could have been realized if the king had imposed on his great vassals the same operation of reconcentration of power which was accomplished regionally. Unfortunately, in 1137, one was still very far from this course, and it may even be doubted that a king like Louis VI could have had even the idea of such an enterprise. Certainly dukes and counts generally gave him homage, although for some of them, especially

From Marcel Pacaut, *Louis VII et son royaume* (Paris, 1964), 258 pages (Work published by the VIe Section de l'Ecole Pratique des Hautes Etudes, 54 rue de Varenne, Paris 7e. Collection: Bibliothéque Générale, en depôt au S.E.V.P.E.N., 13 rue du Four, Paris 6e), pages 12-14, 18, 27-28, 33-34, 36, 39-40, 59-62, 64-65, 67, 117, 119, 122-124, 172-177. Reprinted by permission of the President, Section des Sciences Economiques et Sociales de l'Ecole Pratique des Hautes Etudes. Translated by John B. Henneman.

in the south of the kingdom, the documents are very discreet on this subject. But what did this homage signify? It was first a guarantee for the vassal, the official confirmation of the possession of the fief; then, only a theoretical recognition of royal supremacy, without a clear notion of the reciprocal aspect of the contract...

Four great fiefs—Normandy, Anjou, Blois-Champagne, and Flanders—almost completely encircled the zone of the Capetian domain. They were the best organized of the kingdom; their heads were the most powerful of the royal vassals; they themselves or their predecessors had best known how to undertake and accomplish the work of reconcentration of powers, although in Anjou and Champagne this action was as yet only beginning. The situation of the king was thus difficult; the increase of his power, the extension of his domain, encountered formidable strength on all sides. Above all, he had to fear a coalition against him of these four seigneurs or any three of them. It was necessary to avoid entering into conflict with one of them without being sure of the aid or neutrality of the others. This, in 1137, was the first imperative of the monarchy's policy...

We must not attach excessive importance to what is only theoretical, that is to say, those famous rights of the king. These royal and regalian rights had been effective in the time of Charlemagne and began to become so again in the thirteenth century: monarchical prerogatives over the coinage, fairs and markets, tolls and duties; special power over churches; supreme and permanent authority in matters of justice, and so on. In 1137, certain of these rights were undoubtedly exercised by the monarch, but almost uniquely in the sphere of his domain or in special circumstances. On the other hand, it should be stressed that in the twelfth century, as in earlier epochs, the monarchy continued to appear to the great vassals as a necessary institution... As a practical matter, the powerful lords desired a king because they believed they needed, at the summit of the feudal structure, a guarantor of the system and the rights and duties of each, a supreme arbiter capable, if necessary, of conciliating them, much more than a sovereign judge. Perhaps also because confusedly, they sensed the necessity of keeping among themselves, at the level of the kingdom, a certain cohesion that alone justified the existence of the monarchy.

In addition, the sovereign disposed of more concrete advantages. In the first place, he considered himself, the summit and guarantor of the feudal edifice, as placed above and outside feudalism. If he possessed lands in fief, he did not render homage... Thus he was an extraordinary lord, not being tied to any person in the interior of the kingdom and recognizing no power superior to his own, no more that of the emperor than that of the pope. In the second place, through his coronation he had received a sort of special sacrament that made him an exceptional person established above simple human law and against whom it would be a sacrilege to raise one's hand...

For Louis VII, in effect, kingship, a prestigious function that placed the sovereign far above the other great men of this world, was above all a religious office.

Since he thought that the purpose of all political and social organization consisted in furthering more and more the success of Christian principles and, at best, helping men find their salvation, he reckoned that the job of a king was to oversee the realization of this end from the highest position in the temporal domain. The monarch is, then, in the service of a religious ideal, in the service of Christianity, and, let us even say, in the service of the Church, conceiving the latter in a very broad vision, both mystical and eschatological, and not as the concrete organism for directing Catholicism. It is this idea which led him to protect and endow clerics and churches. It is also this [idea] that would lead him to the crusade and to other enterprises in which kingship and the kingdom had little to gain.

The second element of the "doctrine" of Louis VII was totally different in principle and elaboration. He attached himself to the feudal regime and doubtless was first induced to do so by Suger, who desired to organize French feudalism in a firm way and in a manner by which, in close cohesion, the monarchy was truly the suzerain. To put it another way, the king thought that suzerainty was not a theoretical or purely honorific act conferring on the suzerain rights that were exercised only exceptionally and a role of arbiter that was enacted only at the request of vassals. He judged that this right was a positive fact, that homage ought to be real and to obligate the fief; that is, that it ought to concede to the lord the possibility of action over the fief in cases of nonrespect of the contract of vassalage or the rules of honor then in use ... In 1137, with Louis VII, it was both an idea and a program which reinforced his conception of royal power and gave him, in the name of his mission as lawgiver and guardian of order and peace, the right to intervene truly and obtain aid in these interventions beyond his competence as suzerain ...

The royal initiatives of the first fifteen years of his reign included enterprises carried out in various parts of the kingdom [which were] sometimes brilliant but rarely profitable, as well as the undertaking of the crusade, which placed the Capetian in the first rank of Christian princes. They terminated in an event of a private nature whose political consequences were considerable: the annulment of the king's marriage with Eleanor of Aquitaine ...

Two persons around the king represented opposing tendencies: Suger and Raoul of Vermandois. The first, partisan of peace and order, judged that the Capetian must above all reach an understanding with the count of Champagne; his policy led to adopting a bias in favor of Stephen of Blois in England and Normandy against the projects of the Plantagenets,[1] without taking sides strongly against the latter on this account. The seneschal, Raoul of Vermandois, had more confused ideas. He was no doubt jealous of the count of Champagne, Thibaut IV, and in the palace he was Suger's rival, two sufficient reasons for placing his program in opposition to that of the abbot of Saint-Denis. Besides, by temperament, he pushed for striking actions; he was not a man of peace and negotiation ... The king, because of his character and youth, certainly leaned toward action, that is to say, in favor of Raoul of Vermandois ...

Contemporary witnesses confirm that Louis VII was... an anxious and easily jealous husband ... The scandal broke out in the [Middle] East. The happy mortal who knew how to profit from the favors of the queen was her own uncle, Raymond of Poitiers, prince of Antioch... Louis VII must have suffered cruelly, but he showed himself ready to forget by leaving Antioch and taking the queen, whom he then did not wish to lose, with him by force. However, from that moment the unfaithful spouse herself called for the annulment of her marriage, complaining "to have married a monk" and invoking a tie of consanguinity between herself and her husband, which should have been an impediment to their marriage in 1137... It is certain that after the death of Suger (13 January 1151) [the king] was no longer bound by words of wisdom and no longer impelled toward patience... Besides, he deplored the fact that the queen had given him only two daughters; he was fearful to see in this fact the proof that his marriage was not legitimate and that God did not bless it since He refused him a male heir... An assembly was held at the castle of Beaugency on 21 March 1152 under the presidency of the archbishops of Sens, Reims, Rouen, and Bordeaux. Relatives of the king affirmed on oath the blood-relationship [of the king and queen]; the annulment of the marriage was proclaimed. Eleanor soon returned to Aquitaine. There, in effect, was the corollary of the divorce, and it had been, it seems, one of the reasons for Suger's counsels of patience. Louis VII could not have been unaware of it—with the marriage annulled, he lost all control over that duchy...

In any case, the divorce and remarriage of Eleanor constituted, for Louis, a grave check in the political sphere... At the same time, one must not use it as a reason to denounce the king. [He] had a serious excuse, that of a deceived husband. It was difficult for him to foresee, when he sent his wife away, that [she would] marry... [Henry] Plantagenet, that Eustace[2] would die in the following months, and that by virtue of this fact Henry would become king of England. Now it is only if one adds up all these elements that the divorce takes on the appearance of a political catastrophe. Since it was the divorce alone for which he had taken responsiblity, we can see that he was stricken with bad luck with respect to the rest. [But it] remains that the loss of Aquitaine alone constituted a mistake.

Louis VII certainly was conscious of this and was horrified by the turn taken by events between the spring of 1152 and the fall of 1153. At this moment, as if all abandoned him, he found himself alone to reflect and decide. Suger was dead; Raoul of Vermandois [had] died... in October 1152. In the same period [others] also passed from the scene: Thibaut of Champagne and the count of Flanders, Thierry of Alsace, who left power to his son Philip. Saint Bernard, who had never been among the intimates of the king and whom, it seems, the latter had scarcely liked, was also to end his life in 1153. On all levels, it was necessary to "return to zero," so to speak, to find new men, to define and establish a new policy...

It was not that Louis VII suddenly decided in 1152 to collaborate closely with the Church... [but] with the disappointments of 1152-1154 he took full cognizance of the advantages that an attitude of close *entente* presented to him. In the following years, he adopted this position more deliberately ... We count twenty-three interventions [on behalf of churches] occurring after 1152, as against two before that date. The figures, are, besides, the inverse of those established for the donations—it is during a period when the king is most wary in granting gifts to churches that he grants his protection most easily and reasserts his rights most often. All this denotes a deliberate attitude in the second part of the reign ...

The second opportunity for Louis VII was afforded by the royal domain, whose management he directed intelligently and methodically in the second part of the reign, when he judged the political situation prudently ... Notwithstanding the fact that six properties of appreciable extent were abandoned by him after 1152, ... Louis VII was more parsimonious after this date than before. He was all the more so in the last twenty years of his reign, leading one to believe that he had more clearly taken cognizance of the interests of the domain.

The analysis of the royal acquisitions leads to the same conclusions, as well as illustrating the concern of the sovereign to increase to the maximum his landed power. The acquisitions were, in effect, important. Several great properties were acquired in the second part of his reign ... The most notable fact, moreover, is not the relative importance of these acquisitions but, here again, for those about which the documents are certain, the chronology of their entry into the domain. If one excepts the several properties obtained at dates impossible to determine, one perceives that *all* the acquisitions are after 1152 ...

The last innovation of the years 1150-1154 concerns the profound renovation of the close royal entourage. That is, the people with whom the Capetian governed and who aided him at the time in his policy of collaboration with the clergy, in the exploitation of the domain, and in the administration of justice—above all the officers of the crown.

Among them, the most important was the seneschal, who was first of all the chief of the others and was officially considered the closest collaborator of the monarch. His competence extended to the administration (surveillance and control of the provosts and other local officials), to the army (commander-in-chief in the absence and in place of the king), and to justice (presidency of the *curia* in the sovereign's place). [The seneschal] was, besides, a sort of general majordomo. The position ... had fallen in 1137 to Raoul of Vermandois who had played a great role under Louis VI and remained in office until his death (October 1152). The seneschalship then remained vacant for two years. In 1154 ... it was confided to Thibaut, count of Blois and Chartres, one of the most powerful royal vassals, brother of the count of Champagne. One finds his signature at the bottom of a great number of royal acts, and he was concerned with most of the great business ...

The chancellor was [also] an important man. Officially he had a much more restricted competence than the seneschal since he was charged with drawing up and authenticating royal acts. Besides, always being a cleric, he was occupied with ecclesiastical matters and exercised judicial functions nearly on the same scale as the seneschal. All the same, he was in theory less involved in affairs than the latter. But this was so only in appearance. In fact, [the chancellor] was the personage closest to the monarch, the one who, having custody of the seal, had to have all his confidence, the one who saw [the king] the most often and who, by the compiling of documents, was the best informed of his thoughts, the one, finally, who frequently set the tone of the union between the crown and the church . . . From November 1150, the chancery was directed by the bishop of Soissons, Hugh of Champfleury, who remained in the post until 1172 . . .

Besides these two principal offices, one finds the butler, the chamberlain, and the constable. The butler was specially charged with assisting the monarch in the administration of the domain (among other properties, the vineyards); in this capacity he sometimes took a place in the judicial organization. In 1149, the function was given to Guy III of Senlis and la Tour, who . . . kept it until the end of the reign. At the same time, the direction of the Chamber, which consisted in supervising all that concerned . . . the personal treasure of the king and his family, fell in 1151 to Matthew II of Beaumont, son of his predecessor of the same name who had had it since 1138; Mathew II died in 1175 . . .

It is thus easy to establish that between 1149 and 1154 all the great offices of the crown, with the exception of the constableship, had received new incumbents by reason of death or revocation . . . Louis VII had chosen [his new seneschal] because it was traditional that this office go to a great house, perhaps even to that of Blois, doubtless because [Louis] had to obtain, against the Plantagenet, the friendship and support of his rich neighbors of Blois-Champagne. But it is certain that Thibaut . . . even when he was charged with important missions (justice), never held the place that Raoul had occupied, was never listened to as the latter had been, never had the influence his predecessor had exercised. [Thibaut's] designation was a political act; it aimed at receiving his support and gaining his fidelity. If, on the whole, it gave the anticipated result, it did not completely prevent changes of sides (in 1159, the seneschal was on the side of the Plantagenet). Finally, it left Louis VII freer in his decisions; it permitted him to detach himself a bit from the influence of his traditional entourage . . .

After the death of the count of Vermandois and the abbot of Saint-Denis, there had been a void for several years in the royal entourage. Louis VII was isolated; he had to make hard decision nearly alone, as the absence of well-advised men who could have given him counsel favored the evolution of his own attitudes and led him to reflect at greater length on the given facts of problems. In a word, this matured him. But, at the end of some time, toward about 1160, new counsellors appeared who were going to play a noteworthy role in the last twenty years of his reign . . . This new team, established after 1160, was very different from those at the beginning of the reign. It was formed above all of prelates who represented the best of the high clergy and the directing spheres of the church, and who embodied the deliberate collaboration of the crown with the episcopate ...

Thus, toward 1152, when the great enterprises attempted in the preceding years ... had failed, when dangers accumulated as never before, Louis VII began, in solitude, to take cognizance of his possibilities and his advantages as well as of the perils and inadequacies. He then deliberately accentuated certain tendencies that had already made their appearance: the cooperation with the clergy, the improvement of the royal domain, the reestablishment of monarchical ascendancy, the perfecting of institutions. He thus seized the trumps available to him, while he renounced projects too bold or controversial.

Notes

1. Stephen of Blois, king of England 1135-1154, was a grandson of William the Conqueror whose rights to England and Normandy were challenged by the Plantagenets [Ed.].

2. Eustace, son of Stephen, died in 1153, after which Stephen recognized Henry Plantagenet as heir to the throne of England [Ed.].

Chapter 9 THE GREAT KINGS OF THE DYNASTY

Long regarded as the foremost modern expert on the last century of Capetian rule in France, ROBERT FAWTIER (1995-1966) directed the publication of many important royal financial documents and inventoried the registers of Philip IV's chancery. The best known of his many books and articles is *The Capetian Kings of France,* a short but brilliant synthesis describing the monarchy between 987 and 1328. The following selection is taken from that volume.

Louis VI built wisely and profitably on the foundations laid by his father. He relied on the Church, and defended it, and secured its support in return. And the current of history was running in his favour. Throughout France the greater nobles were tending to devote themselves more and more to improving the internal organisation of their fiefs. Thus preoccupied, they wanted to live at peace with each other and with the king. They saw that a victory of the Anglo-Norman royal house over the Capets would endanger their own interests ...

Fortune was on his side in another field. His reign fell in the period when the townspeople of France were organising themselves in communes. Like all the feudal

From Robert Fawtier, *The Capetian Kings of France,* translated by L. Butler and R. J. Adam (London, New York, and Toronto, 1960), pp. 20-31. Reprinted by permission of St. Martin's Press, Inc., the Macmillan Company of Canada, and the Macmillan Company of London and Basingstoke.

lords of his time, Louis had been induced to issue or confirm charters recognising the new communes and granting them privileges. This was enough to persuade the great romantic historians to represent him as a friend of the common people of France, an opinion which, though by now severely shaken and all but demolished, still faintly influences the views of modern scholars. The king whom Suger praised has always commanded the sympathy of historians; and he is one of those rare monarchs whose name lives on in popular memory.

The real Louis VI was an active king, and intelligent enough, it seems, to make use of the favourable circumstances in which he found himself. In the royal domain he did no more than pursue vigorously the traditional policy of Robert the Pious [Robert II], Henry I and Philip I, whose activities there, as traced by the specialists who have studied their reigns, look like preliminary sketches for the work Louis was to accomplish. But if Louis fitted into an old tradition and reigned at the opportune time for reaping its benefits, he must take credit for not breaking it and for handing on to his successors a royal domain almost completely pacified. His reputation has been enhanced by his courage as well as his success. For biographer he had one of the most appealing—perhaps because one of the very few well-known—figures of his age. Everything needed to win him the esteem of his contemporaries and of posterity was his.

His son and successor, Louis VII (r. 1137-1180), though less well endowed by fortune, was more attractive in personality . . .

Historians have been surprisingly slow to appreciate Louis VII at his true worth; and yet . . . in Louis VII's reign the prestige of the French monarchy was decisively established, and began to grow steadily. Louis was a realist. He grasped the need to assure the succession to the throne and to carry on the traditional policy of his dynasty in the royal domain . . .

Louis was a loyal servant of the Church. When Pope Alexander III was driven from Italy by the Emperor Frederick Barbarossa, Louis gave him shelter and refuge, and treated him with extreme deference. But he displayed no weakness when the royal rights over the Church were called in question; and he was able to make use of the Papacy in his conflict with Henry II of England.

The difficulties which confronted Louis VII are easily underrated. During his reign a feudal principality of unprecedented strength grew up within the borders of his kingdom. By his marriage in 1152 with Eleanor of Aquitaine, Louis' ex-wife, Henry II added the entire duchy of Aquitaine to his inherited fiefs of Normandy and Anjou. Shortly afterwards, in 1154, he became King of England. Louis VII strove to the best of his ability with this formidable new power. At times he blundered. But in his struggle to make use of the feuds within the Anglo-Norman royal family and to exploit his own position as feudal suzerain and his prestige as anointed king, he was at least working out a policy for dealing with his dangerous rival which in the hands of his son Philip Augustus [Philip II] was to win a great victory for the House of Capet. At the very time when Louis' situation was at its most critical, the bishops of the south of France turned to him and sought his protection. It may well have been that the shrewdest way of dealing with the Angevin danger looming over his dynasty was to go on playing the part of the pious, gentle king, bearing malevolence to no man, and ruling in harmony with the intellectual currents of the age.

On the other hand, Louis has been severely criticised, especially by French historians, for himself creating the Angevin menace by repudiating Eleanor of Aquitaine as his wife. Yet it is by no means clear that to repudiate Eleanor was a mistake. In 1137 the French monarchy was hardly ready to assimilate the huge duchy of Aquitaine, whose feudatories were among the most turbulent in Europe. Draw as they might on their own portentous energies, and on the resources of England, Normandy, and Anjou, Henry II and Richard I could never subdue Aquitaine. The attempt to keep order there would have exhausted the Capetian monarchy, backed as it was by only its incompletely pacified little royal domain, and harassed as it must have been by great vassals seeking to profit from the monarchy's new preoccupation with expeditions to the south. The beautiful Eleanor's misconduct while on crusade at Antioch, if indeed it was Louis' true reason for divorcing her, was providential for the monarchy. Having lost his wife, Louis made a serious but short-lived effort to keep a hold on her lands and to stop her second marriage. He achieved neither purpose: perhaps because, in the long run, he lacked the will to do so, or descried too clearly the risks involved. Certainly the means at his disposal were inadequate. Despite appearances, the Capetian monarchy in 1152 was still a long way from being a great power, and was only to attain that status under Louis VII's successor.

Philip II (1180-1223) was the great king of the Capetian dynasty, and its exemplar long after his death. As a youth he seems to have taken after his grandfather Louis VI. There was the same corpulence, the vitality, the combativeness. Hard experience, early undergone—for he was king at fourteen, and at twenty-five, while on crusade in Palestine, he had a terrible illness . . . turned him into a cautious, cynical, distrustful man, and left him with a sickly nervousness of disposition which he usually had the strength of will to master. Phillip's intellectual gifts were modest: he tried and failed to learn Latin; but he had a keen practical intelligence and was capable of making plans on a large scale and of executing them with a painstaking energy which ensured their success. His grandson, St. Louis [Louis IX], who was nine years old when Philip died, told his friend Joinville of a conversation he had had with the old king: 'He said to me that a king should reward his men strictly in proportion to the services they had done him, and that no man could become a good ruler who was incapable of being as firm in refusing as he was generous in giving.' St. Louis' own dying words to his son—as Joinville reports them—were: 'Once upon a time one of the counsellors of my grandfather Philip insisted to him that the clergy were doing him grave wrongs, encroaching on his royal rights and obstructing his justices, and that it was astounding that he should put up with such treatment. The good old king answered that he believed this to be true, but that considering all the favours God had shown him, he would rather forfeit royal rights than quarrel with God's priests.'

If there was no irony behind this second adage of Philip Augustus (and we have no evidence that there was) it lends admirable support to the first. Philip was a hard master, but he endeavoured to do justice to both God and man. His subjects were bound to do him good service, indeed this was in his eyes their sole function; and he readily acknowledged his duty to reward them for it—but the reward must be closely commensurate with the services rendered. And this was how a great king should think and behave. Yet he must set an example and himself be the foremost and most devoted servant of the crown. Especially in the latter part of his career did Philip Augustus act on these principles. He was tirelessly active, a brave and daring war leader, a prudent and skilful diplomat, reorganising his kingdom internally after a fashion that influenced the character of the French monarchy for centuries.

It must be admitted that good luck was on his side. A crossbowman's bolt rid him in the nick of time of his most dangerous enemy, Richard the Lion Heart of England; and no one could accuse Philip of having had any hand in this fortunate accident. Thanks to the unbridled savagery of Richard's successor, John Lackland, the young Arthur of Brittany was removed from the scene, and with him the possibility of a strong opposition, supported by the nobility, to Philip's absorption of the Plantagenet inheritance on the continent.[1] King John's blundering drove the English barons into revolt at the very time when a united England might have proved fatal to Philip. [Pope] Innocent III's veto prevented Philip from embarking personally on the risky gamble of an attempted conquest of England. Innocent's policies also brought into the field against the Albigensian heretics the most adventurous spirits among the feudal nobility of France north of the Loire. From their conquest of the Midi the French monarchy was the ultimate gainer. Still, Philip was the man to turn Fortune's bounties, 'God's favours', to profit. On the field of Bouvines[2] he was the heroic king in action, the courageous knightly leader. In the field of diplomacy he deployed a marvellous skill in his dealings with John Lackland and Arthur, with the English barons, with the Holy See. He was a master of legal argument, seizing on every advantagcontrol effectively a vast royal domain. St. Louis' dictum 'There is only one king in France' was true from the reign of Philip Augustus onwards... The speedy rise of the Capetian monarchy which Philip's exertions and his good luck had brought about would have been an ephemeral thing if his successors had been mediocre or incompetent; but few of them were mediocrities, and some were great kings. With Philip's example before it, the dynasty held fast to what he had accomplished.

King Louis VIII (r. 1223-1226) successfully carried on the work Philip had begun. But Louis lacked his father's physical stamina, and burnt himself out in a forty-months' reign of unresting activity. His premature death came at the high tide of success, when he had just victoriously established royal power in Poitou and Languedoc. Languedoc had been all but independent, and but for Louis VIII the crusade against the Albigensian heretics might have put power there in the hands of a new feudal dynasty even harder to subdue than the old line of the counts of Toulouse.

The hour that struck the death of Louis VIII was arguably the most critical in the history of the Capetian family. The new king, one day to be St. Louis, was still a child. The trend of events in the previous two reigns had brought the higher nobility to realise that its independence would soon be seriously threatened. But a unique opportunity for a counterblow had now arisen. And so opposition was raised to the regency of the queen-mother, Blanche of Castile, on the pretext that she was a woman and a foreigner...[This] was not the first occasion on which the king's widow had acted as regent, nor the first on which a queen had played a part in politics... But Blanche of Castile was to play a greater role than any of her predecessors. To all intents and purposes she may be counted among the kings of France. For from 1226 until her death in 1252 she governed the kingdom... Taking her father-in-law, Philip Augustus, as her model, she won over half her enemies by craft, vigorously gave battle to the rest, and enlisted the alliance of the Church, including the Pope himself, and of the burgess class, which in marked fashion took the side of the royal family. Blanche was able to fend off King Henry III of England, who tried to take the opportunity of recovering his ancestral lands, lost by John to Philip Augustus. She broke up the baronial coalition and reduced to submission the most dangerous of the rebels, Peter Mauclerc, Count of Brittany, and Raymond VII, Count of Toulouse. She adroitly took advantage of her victory to reestablish—this time definitively—the royal power in the south of France—her son Alphonse was married to the daughter and heiress of Raymond of Toulouse. The way was now open for the union of all Raymond's rich patrimony with the royal domain.

The Capetian monarchy emerged all the stronger from a crisis which had threatened to overwhelm it...

But what posterity most remembers Blanche of Castile for is that she gave birth to and brought up Louis IX, the king who won and kept first place in French affections, who most strongly influenced the development of the French monarchy, and who obscured the glory of his forerunners and successors alike. After his time, men spoke not of the Capetians, of the royal house of France, of the throne of France: but of the line of St. Louis, the blood of St. Louis, and the throne of St. Louis.

In his youth Louis IX (r. 1226-1270) was a handsome knightly figure, slender and upstanding, with the face of an angel lit up by 'the eyes of a dove.' The man of mature years was an ascetic, his body wearied by the mortifying penances he inflicted upon it; yet all who came near him felt his unforgettable charm. Louis was simple in manner and dress, generally jovial, though capable of violent anger, and fundamentally good-natured, but with a zeal for justice which could, when the occasion demanded, arouse in him the energies called for in a great king. He was a dutiful son—probably too much so for the taste of his ambitious wife, Margaret of Provence. He well understood the greatness of his mother's achievement, and sagaciously allowed her to govern the realm as long as she wished; but this is not to say that Louis was anxious to unload the burdens of kingship on to Blanche or that he had no will of his own. On the contrary, no King of France seems to have taken his high office more conscientiously. Kingship for him was not a mere opportunity of lording it over other men, or making his subjects happy, or conquering other kingdoms, or feathering his own nest. He approached it—as he approached everything else—with his Christian faith as his guide, a faith which was his lifelong inspiration, and was founded not on convictions reached through theological ponderings, but on the deep and sure belief that lies beyond all questionings and is marked by the tranquil joy which only those who experience religious certainty can know. Had Louis been born into a different social station, he would have taken vows and become a monk. He thought of so doing, indeed, but was restrained by his sense of the duties of kingship. God had put him on the throne, he believed, to serve the Christian faith and to lead his people not to worldly happiness but toward eternal salvation.

Such an idea, held by a king of different calibre, would have put the monarchy on the road to ruin. But it was not for nothing that St. Louis had listened to the counsel of his grandfather Philip Augustus—whom he freely quoted. Not for nothing had he come under the influence of the pious Blanche of Castile. Blanche is credited with the awe-inspiring remark that she would sooner see her son dead than cure him at the price of a mortal sin. She taught Louis that a man may sin not only in his own person but also through another, that the sins of the subject become the sins of the king, and that no king can be without sin if his subjects live in iniquity. Now to lead the people out of their life of sin, a king must be strong and command obedience. With faith as his guide, he can and should take all decisions upon himself. And so an absolute monarch can, alone, lead his people to salvation. Reasoning thus, Louis IX sought to make the French monarchy absolute. (He could hardly have foreseen the ultimately disastrous consequences of absolutism.) An absolute monarchy is perhaps what Philip Augustus had desired. Philip the Fair [Philip IV], Louis' grandson and faithful admirer, was to work towards the same goal, as were other French kings of the future, striving towards the same goal, as were other French kings of the future, striving towards that ideal of monarchy by divine right which Louis XIV was most fully to represent. But the motives which worked upon these more or less conscious architects of absolutism were not those which fired St. Louis. The others thought of their kingdom or of themselves. St. Louis thought of the immortal souls of the men he ruled.

Notes

1. John "Lackland," king of England 1199-1216, had a rival in his nephew Arthur, count of Brittany, but had Arthur murdered in 1203 [Ed.].

2. The battle of Bouvines, fought in the summer of 1214, was a decisive victory for Philip II over the allies of John of England [Ed.].

Chapter 10: LOUIS IX, THE EMBODIMENT OF MORALITY AND JUSTICE

JEAN DE JOINVILLE (1224-1317), ten years younger than Louis IX, was seneschal of Champagne in the thirteenth century. He accompanied the king on the first of his crusades and became his good friend. Sixty years after this crusade, Joinville composed his famous biography of the sainted king. He wrote a frank and honest appraisal of a man he liked and admired but did not fear to criticize or disagree with. It tells us what it was that members of the aristocracy admired in Louis IX and provides a valuable insight into the values and attitudes of the thirteenth century French nobility as well as the king himself.

This holy man loved God with all his heart, and followed Him in His acts; and thus appeared in that, as God died for the love He bore His people, so did the king put his body in peril, and that several times, for the love he bore to his people; and such peril he might well have avoided, as you shall be told hereafter.

The great love that he bore to his people appeared in what he said during a very sore sickness that he had at Fontainebleau, unto my Lord Louis, his eldest son. "Fair son," he said, "I pray thee to make thyself beloved of the people of thy kingdom; for truly I would rather that a Scot should come out of Scotland and

From the book *Mémoirs of the Crusades* by Villehardouin and De Joinville, pp. 139-141, 149-152. Published in New York in 1958 by E. P. Dutton & Co., Inc., in paperback and reprinted with their permission. This paperback edition is based on the Everyman's Library Text, and permission to reprint these extracts in the British Commonwealth has been granted also by J. M. Dent & Sons Ltd. of London.

govern the people of the kingdom well and equitably than that thou shouldest govern it ill in the sight of all men." The holy king so loved truth, that as you shall hear hereafter, he would never consent to lie to the Saracens as to any covenant that he had made with them.

Of his mouth he was so sober, that on no day of my life did I ever hear him order special meats, as many rich men are wont to do; but he ate patiently whatever his cooks had made ready, and was set before him. In his words he was temperate; for on no day of my life did I ever hear him speak evil of any one; nor did I ever hear him name the Devil—which name is very commonly spoken throughout the kingdom, whereby God, as I believe, is not well pleased.

He asked me if I wished to be honoured in this world, and to go into paradise at my death? And I said "Yes." And he said: "Keep yourself then from knowingly doing or saying anything which, if the whole world heard thereof, you would be ashamed to acknowledge, saying 'I did this,' or 'I said that.'" He told me to beware not to contradict or impugn anything that was said before me—unless indeed silence would be a sin or to my own hurt—because hard words often move to quarrelling, wherein men by the thousand have found death.

He said that men ought to clothe and arm their bodies in such wise that men of worth and age would never say, this man has done too much, nor young men say, this man has done too little. And I repeated this saying to the father of the king that now is, when speaking of the embroidered coats of arms that are made nowadays; and I told him that never, during our voyage oversea, had I seen embroidered coats, either belonging to the king or to any one else. And the king that now is told me that he had such suits, with arms embroidered, as had cost him eight hundred pounds *parisis*. And I told him he would have employed the money to better purpose if he had given it to God, and had had his suits made of good taffeta (satin) ornamented with his arms, as his father had done.

He called me once to him and said: "Because of the subtle mind that is in you I dare not speak to you of the things relating to God; so I have summoned these two monks that are here, as I want to ask you a question." Now the question was this: "Seneschal," said he, "what manner of thing is God?" And I said: "Sire, it is so good a thing that there cannot be better." "Of a truth," said he, "you have answered well; for the answer that you have given is written in this book that I hold in my hand."

"Now I ask you," said he, "which you would the better like, either to be a leper, or to have committed a mortal sin?" And I, who never lied to him, made answer that I would rather have committed thirty mortal sins than be a leper. And when the monks had departed, he called me to him alone, and made me sit at his feet, and said, "How came you to say that to me yesterday?" And I told him that I said it again. And he answered, "You spoke hastily and as a fool. For you should know that there is no leprosy so hideous as the being in mortal sin, inasmuch as the soul that is in mortal sin is like unto the Devil; wherefore no leprosy can be so hideous. And sooth it is that, when a man dies, he is healed of the leprosy in his body; but when a man who has committed mortal sin dies, he cannot know of a certainty that he has, during his lifetime, repented in such sort that God has forgiven him; wherefore he must stand in great fear lest that leprosy of sin should last as long as God is in paradise. So I pray you," said he, "as strongly as I can, for the love of God, and for the love of me, so to set your heart that you prefer any evil that can happen to the body, whether it be leprosy, or any other sickness, rather than that mortal sin should enter into your soul."

He asked me if I washed the feet of the poor on Holy Thursday. "Sire," said I, "it would make me sick! The feet of these villains will I not wash." "In truth," said he, "that was ill said; for you should never disdain what God did for our teaching. So I pray you, for the love of God first, and then for the love of me, that you accustom yourself to wash the feet of the poor" ...

A gray-friar (Franciscan) came to him at the castle of Hyères, there where we disembarked; and said in his sermon, for the king's instruction, that he had read the Bible, and the books pertaining to heathen princes, and that he had never found, either among believers or misbelievers, that a kingdom had been lost, or had changed lords, save there had first been failure of justice. "Therefore let the king, who is going into France, take good heed," said he, "that he do justice well and speedily among his people, so that our Lord suffer his kingdom to remain in peace all the days of his life." It is said that the right worthy man who thus instructed the king, lies buried at Marseilles, where our Lord, for his sake, performs many a fine miracle. He would never consent to remain with the king, however much the king might urge it, for more than a single day.

The king forgot not the teaching of the friar, but ruled his land very loyally and godly, as you shall hear. He had so arranged that my Lord of Nesle, and the good Count of Soissons, and all of us who were about him, should go, after we had heard our masses, and hear the pleadings at the gate which is now called the gate of Requests.
hear the pleadings at the gate which is now called the gate of Requests.

And when he came back from church, he would send for us and sit at the foot of his bed, and make us all sit round him, and ask if there were any whose cases could not be settled save by himself in person. And we named the litigants; and he would then send for such and ask: "Why do you not accept what our people offer?" And they would make reply, "Sire, because they offer us very little." Then would he say, "You would do well to accept what is proposed, as our people desire." And the saintly man endeavoured thus, with all his power, to bring them into a straight path and a reasonable.

Ofttimes it happened that he would go, after his mass, and seat himself in the wood of Vincennes, and lean against an oak, and make us sit round him. And all those who had any cause in hand came and spoke to him, without hindrance of usher, or of any other person. Then would he ask, out of his own mouth, "Is there any one who has a cause in hand?" And those who had a cause in hand stood up. Then would he say, "Keep silence all, and you shall be heard in turn, one after the other." Then he would call my Lord Peter of Fontaines and my Lord Geoffry of Villette,[1] and say to one of them, "Settle me this cause."

And when he saw that there was anything to amend in the words of those who spoke on his behalf, or in the words of those who spoke on behalf of any other person, he would himself, out of his own mouth, amend what they had said. Sometimes have I seen him, in summer, go to do justice among his people in the garden of Paris, clothed in a tunic of camlet, a surcoat of tartan without sleeves, and a mantle of black taffeta about his neck, his hair well combed, no cap, and a hat of white peacock's feathers upon his head. And he would cause a carpet to be laid down, so that we might sit round him, and all the people who had any cause to bring before him stood around. And then would he have their causes settled, as I have told you afore he was wont to do in the wood of Vincennes.

I saw him, yet another time, in Paris, when all the prelates of France had asked to speak with him, and the king went to the palace to give them audience. And there was present Guy of Auxerre, the son of my Lord William of Mello, and he spoke to the king on behalf of all the prelates, after this manner: "Sire, the lords who are here present, archbishops and bishops, have directed me to tell you that Christendom, which ought to be guarded and preserved by you, is perishing in your hands." The king crossed himself when he heard that word, and he said, "Tell me how that may be."

"Sire," said Guy of Auxerre, "it is because excommunications are at the present day so lightly thought of that people suffer themselves to die before seeking absolution, and will not give satisfaction to the Church. These lords require you therefore, for the sake of God, and because it is your duty, to command your provosts and baliffs to seek out all such as suffer themselves to remain excommunicated for a year and day, and constrain them, by seizure of their goods, to have themselves absolved."

And the king replied that he would issue such commands willingly whensoever it could be shown to him that the excommunicate persons were in the wrong. The bishops said they would accept this condition at no price whatever, as they contested his jurisdiction in their causes. Then the king told them he would do no other; for it would be against God and reason if he constrained people to seek absolution when the clergy were doing them wrong. "And of this," said the king, "I will give you an example, viz., that of the Count of Brittany, who, for seven years long, being excommunicated, pleaded against the prelates of Brittany, and carried his cause so far that the Apostle (the Pope) condemned them all. Wherefore, if I had constrained the Count of Brittany, at the end of the first year, to get himself absolved, I should have sinned against God and against him." Then the prelates resigned themselves; nor did I ever hear tell that any further steps were taken in the aforesaid matters.

The peace that he made with the King of England was made against the advice of his council, for the council said to him: "Sire, it seems to us that you are giving away the land that you make over to the King of England; for he has no right thereto, seeing that his father lost it justly." To this the king replied that he knew well that the King of England had no right to the land, but that there was a reason why he should give it him, "for," said he, "we have two sisters to wife, and our children are cousins-german; wherefore it is fitting that there should be peace between us. Moreover a very great honour accrues to me through the peace that I have made with the King of England, seeing that he is now my liegeman, which he was not aforetime."

The uprightness of the king may be seen in the case of my lord Renaud of Trie, who brought to the saintly man a charter stating that the king had given to the heirs of the Countess of Boulogne, lately deceased, the county of Dammartin in Gouelle. The seal on the charter was broken, so that naught remained save half the legs of the image on the king's seal, and the stool on which the king set his feet. And the king showed the seal to all those who were of his council, and asked us to help him to come to a decision. We all said, without a dissentient, that he was not bound to give effect to the charter. Then he told John Sarrasin, his chamberlain, to give him a charter which he had asked him to obtain. When he held this charter in his hands, he said: "Lords, this is the seal I used before I went overseas, and you can see clearly from this seal that the impression on the broken seal is like unto that of the seal that is whole; wherefore I should not dare, in good conscience, to keep the said county." So he called to him my lord Renaud of Trie, and said, "I give you back the county."

Note

1. These two lords were important royal judicial officers [Ed].

Chapter 11 THE EMERGENCE OF PROVINCIAL ADMINISTRATION

JAMES W. FESLER (b. 1911), Cowles Professor of Government at Yale University, has specialized in the study of comparative political systems in Europe and the United States. Written from the perspective of a political scientist, the article from which this selection is taken is one of the best concise statements of early royal provincial administration in France.

In the six centuries preceding the Revolution, French field administration was built around the royal bailiffs and seneschals, who first appeared in the late twelfth century and became firmly established as resident field agents in the thirteenth century. The period of the system's founding was characterized by prosperity, by expansion of the kingdom and the royal proprietary domain, by mounting governmental expenditures, and by able rulers. By 1328 the royal domain was forty times its size in the year 1000, and the major gains had occurred in the thirteenth century. The population of the kingdom of France approached 20 million. Expenditures from the royal treasury were perhaps seven times greater toward the end of the thirteenth century than at its start . . .

From James W. Fesler, "French Field Administration: The Beginnings," *Comparative Studies in Society and History*, V (1962), pp. 79-80, 82-83, 85-86, 93-94, 96-102. Reprinted by permission of the author and the Cambridge University Press. Footnotes omitted.

Some time after the middle of the twelfth century bailiffs and seneschals were added to the provostship system of French field administration. "Bailiff" was the term generally preferred, especially in what was then the king's domain or "France proper," as distinguished from southern and western France, where great additions to the domain shortly occurred and where the term "seneschal" was widely employed for substantially the same post as that of "bailiff" elsewhere. For convenience, we shall use "bailiff" as a generic term, covering both bailiffs and seneschals, save where distinctive reference to seneschals is necessary . . .

At first the bailiffs were stationed at Paris and sent out as members of the king's Court to tour a group of provostships. Later they took up residence in their assigned areas and more and more became the hierarchical superiors of the provosts. In the first stage they in effect carried the king's Court to local areas and brought back to the king their impressions and informed counsel. Yet their functions were more than merely inspection and reporting. They also had judicial, financial, political, and administrative functions, a reflection not just of specific authorization by the king but as well of the fact that they represented a central Court that itself had not yet differentiated its functions.

Four descriptive facts are basic. (1) The bailiffs had the prestige of membership in the Court. (2) They were "outsiders," not local residents with ties of affection and self-interest in the area visited. (3) Their areas of tour were groups of provostships, to be known as bailiwicks, which, of course, meant larger field areas than those of any other existing field officials. (4) They went out to the assigned bailiwicks not singly, but in pairs or in groups . . . Whatever the motives for its institution, the system of touring groups of bailiffs lasted less than fifty years. The system was gradually modified by singularizing the bailiffs so that each bailiwick had only one bailiff, and by physically stationing the bailiffs in their assigned bailiwicks. It is this regularized scheme of field administration that was to serve the monarchy for centuries and that therefore particularly warrants our attention . . .

Probably nothing was more effective in divorcing bailiffs from identification with local interests than the policy of restricting the length of time an individual could serve in a particular bailiwick. Along with this rather mechanical principle was appropriately linked the development of a primitive kind of administrative career service. In principle there appears to have been a three-year limit on service in any one bailiwick. This limit was not observed strictly, for cases can be cited of men serving twelve, fourteen, nineteen, twenty-five years in the same bailiwicks. But the emphasis should be on the wide adherence to the principle, rather than on the striking exceptions. In Normandy, most of the bailiffs of the thirteenth century served at their posts less than five years. In Vermandois in the North and in Beaucaire in the South, the predominant pattern was short tenure. Furthermore, the pattern becomes firmer in the later part of the period: the exceptions generally concern men already well settled in particular bailiwicks before mid-century or men appointed before the end of Saint Louis's reign in 1270.

The career-service principle can be illustrated by the cases of particular bailiffs. The most famous bailiff from the vantage point of the twentieth century, a judgment affected by his literary and juristic contributions, was Philippe de Beaumanoir ... A native of Beauvais, just north of Paris, and "of a good family," he spent part of his youth in England and Scotland, and became bailiff of Clermont, which had been granted as an appanage to Robert, one of Saint Louis's younger sons. Transferring to the king's own service, and with the benefit of legal training, Beaumanoir served successively as bailiff or seneschal in Poitou and Limousin, Saintonge, Vermandois, Touraine, and Senlis. The geographic range of his career is notable. In Poitou, Limousin, and Saintonge he was a southern "seneschal"; in Vermandois and Senlis, both north of Paris, and in Touraine to the west, he was a northern "bailiff." On the side he wrote the *Coutumes de Beauvaisis,* which crystallized the general principles of French customary law in the North (in contrast to the written law of the South) ...

The functions of the bailiff were those of an administrative generalist, or perhaps *governmental* generalist would be more accurate, for judicial, financial, even quasi-military functions, as well as ordinary administrative functions, were embraced in his assignment. Where their itinerant predecessor bailiffs had brought the Court to the locality, the bailiffs stationed in the field had something of the quality of, literally, viceroys. "There, where they are, it seems that the king himself is."

While the most notable feature of the responsibilities of the bailiff was their broad scope, these responsibilities did not comprehend the full range of the king's interests in the bailiwick, nor were they performed without supervision and intervention by central officials. These qualifications need to be noted, for it is all too easy to be victimized by the rhetorical view of generalist field agents as "little kings." In fact, the bailiffs were hierarchical subordinates not only of the king (which, of course, need not preclude the king's having other subordinates in the field), but as well of administrative bodies and officials at Paris. For it was in the thirteenth and early fourteenth centuries that the royal government ceased to be the highly personal affair of the king and his Court, the latter loosely composed of whatever great nobles, ecclesiastics, and officers of the king's household happened to be in attendance at a given time.

The foundations of modern government were laid by growth within the Court of (a) a small privy council, called the Great Council, composed of salaried "king's men" and advising in secret sessions on high policy matters, whether foreign or domestic, financial or administrative; (b) the *Parlement,* with primarily judicial functions; (c) the Chamber of Accounts, for financial functions; and (d) the Chancery, constituting the king's secretariat, and headed by the Chancellor who was destined to become the hub of royal government. Membership overlapped among these bodies, to be sure, and the fiction was retained for some time that the *curia regis,* the king's Court, was the body making or confirming decisions, assisted and facilitated by committees of its members ...

The Parlement, though eventually to play an historic role in resistance to absolutism, is not to be confused with law-making parliaments. Its distinctive emphasis was judicial. Despite the medieval emphasis on the king himself as the source of justice, the Parlement was authorized to make binding decisions on behalf of the king and his court. The king's participation became only a myth, as he rarely attended. By the year 1250 the Parlement sat only at Paris instead of accompanying the king on his tours of the kingdom.

The judicial role of the bailiffs was marked out by the range of the royal jurisdiction and by the definition of the Parlement's special role. On his own proprietary domain the king's jurisdiction was, of course, incontestable, and it was on that domain that his provosts heard minor disputes and judged misdemeanors and his bailiffs held assizes and heard appeals from the decisions of provosts and other inferior officials. But within the lands that were the domains of feudal lords, the situation was different. In such a domain the lord himself had powers of "high justice" and maintained his own courts, often in complex hierarchies. In those courts were heard the criminal cases and the civil disputes between the lord's vassals. The king's central court had original jurisdiction of disputes between great lords or between the king and any of the lords; for example, it was this court that declared King John of England's great continental holdings forfeit when John (a vassal of the French king) refused to appear to answer Philip Augustus's charges. Expansion of the royal jurisdiction, a critical development in the undermining of feudalism, depended upon the king's courts' (a) taking original jurisdiction of cases involving certain kinds of parties (e.g. where the parties were vassals of different feudal lords, or where one of them was a vassal on the royal domain or a royal official such as a bailiff), (b) asserting original jurisdiction regardless of parties where the matter in dispute involved a right or license granted by the king; and (c) providing a right of appeal from the feudal lords' court to the royal courts.

The unremitting efforts of bailiffs to extend the *original* jurisdiction of the king's justice were vital to the insinuation of direct royal rule into all the fiefs of France. Yet the perfecting of *appellate* jurisdiction both supplemented and regulated those efforts. In medieval times an appeal was against the judge rather than against the other party in the case. Grounds for appeal were either denial of justice, such as the judge's refusal to hear a case, or error of judgment, the assumption being that a judge's error in deciding a case could not but be deliberate. Yet an ordinary party to a case might in fact be unqualified to hale a judge before an appellate court. So long as trial by combat was a common way of settling on whose side "Right" lay when error of judgment was charged and so long as noble and non-noble persons could not appropriately fight each other, the resort to appellate courts would clearly be restricted. No wonder that Montesquieu hailed Saint Louis's abolition of trial by combat and substitution of proof by evidence as "a kind of revolution," broadening as it did the opportunities to appeal decisions thought erroneous.

Appeals, then, might be taken from feudal lords' courts to the royal courts, and, assuming the full gamut of lords' courts had been run, the appeals would be addressed to the Parlement itself. Appeals from bailiffs' decisions were also directed there. Increasingly the Parlement found itself occupied with its appellate jurisdiction, which had significant nationalizing effects. As Ferdinand Lot and Robert Fawtier put it, "The exercise of the right of appeal contributed, more than all concerted policy, to the formation of French unity."

Its appellate role had the result, important for our purposes, of interposing the Parlement as a "functional supervisor" of the bailiffs in their judicial capacities. So much was this true that the bailiffs, when appointed, took one of their oaths of office before the Parlement ... At the same time, Parlement strengthened the bailiff's jurisdiction by insisting, especially as its own load of work mounted, that the hierarchy of lower courts be traversed and that a litigant unhappy with an adverse judgment by a bailiff petition the bailiff for a reconsideration of his decision. A further link between the Parlement and the bailiffs was that the king's decrees became legally binding for bailiffs in their capacities as judges and enforcement officers only upon their "registration" with the Parlement ...

One is tempted to hurry along the move toward modernity represented by differentiation of functions. But before differentiation there was blending of functions supported not only by tradition but by a logic whose force is likely to be overlooked by the impatient. Consider the interconnection between the administration of justice and the collection of revenue. Every revenue administration action had about it a judicial character; every judicial action had about it a revenue aspect. Tax collectors, such as the bailiffs, were asserters of the validity of the king's law and judges both of what taxes were owed by individuals under that law and of what penalties were collectible from those resisting payment. Each collector in turn was accountable to the central government, whose Court would verify or "judge" whether the amount turned in fulfilled the collector's obligation to his king.

The other side of the coin is that justice itself was a revenue-yielding function. The payment of damages called for by a decision benefited not only the aggrieved party; the amounts were shared by the king as the provider of royal justice. Furthermore, extension of the king's judicial reach beyond his own proprietary domain inevitably stretched his financial grasp. For example, when a vassal of a feudal lord alleged in a royal court that his lord's courts had denied him justice, the vassal's obligations to his lord were suspended and he was taken under the king's protection until the royal courts might dispose of the case. If the lord then moved against his vassal he was subjected to a heavy fine. Thus royal jurisdiction might be established in the heart of a lord's domain and if it were questioned the king would profit financially. In these circumstances it is not surprising that some appeals were allowed to drag on for many years.

The financial functions of the bailiffs and their subordinates, especially the provosts, consisted of the collection of *regular* revenue and the expenditure of funds for local activities. From the collections were paid the salaries and wages of the bailiwick's field staff, the costs of such local undertakings as maintenance and repair of local roads and royal castles, and the charities and individual grants that a generous and importuned king authorized for the benefit of particular institutions and persons in the bailiwick. Only the balance remaining after these direct local expenditures was transmitted to Paris.

Particularly in financial matters the complexities of a three-tiered hierarchy—Paris, bailiff, and provost—worked out slowly in the thirteenth century ... The bailiff was a salaried, responsible royal official, while the provost typically bought his post at auction as a "farm." In due course the provosts lost their Paris connection and came to transmit the due amounts directly to their bailiffs, while the bailiff's accounts as submitted to Paris were so organized as to identify the revenues of each provostship. On the local expenditures side as well, responsibilities tended to shift from provost to bailiff ...

Delivery of funds to Paris every few months, and verification of accounts there, provided important opportunities for field agents to be reminded of their responsibilities, to renew their identification with the central government, and to absorb a sense of royal policy. Originally presenting their accounts to the king in Court, the bailiffs by the early 1300's were instead dealing with the Chamber of Accounts. A significant evolution in accountability had taken place during this period. The king's Court had first obtained the aid of a committee on accounts made up of designated members of the Court. The committee met several times each year, for two or three weeks at a time, in order to check the accounts of the Knights Templar,[1] whose Temple at Paris was not only a bank, but served as the royal treasury in which field agents and other officials deposited their collections and from which issued the funds for authorized expenditures. The Court committee was in turn aided by a subcommittee that continuously through the year checked accounts in preparation for the main committee's meetings. In 1303, as a consequence of Philip the Fair's vigorous attack on the Knights Templar, the subcommittee took up quarters in the Palace, alongside the king, the Parlement, and other royal officers and agencies of the Court. The subcommittee's room (*chambre*) became known as the Chamber of Accounts. The "Master of Accounts" (*Maîtres des comptes*) rapidly developed such specialized competence that they were soon rid of the higher ecclesiastics and nobles who had hitherto attempted to share in the work. So Court, committee, and subcommittee had given way to professionals.

Except for the Great Council, the Chamber of Accounts was to become in the fourteenth century "by far the most important organ of the monarchy, superior even to the Parlement." It is then "the factotum of royalty because, in a general administration with contours as yet imprecise, the Chamber of Accounts, lodged at the Palace, beside the sovereign, is the only *corps* of the State that is established, organized and continuous." Although only twenty to thirty persons constituted the Chamber, their competence, the constantly critical state of the royal finances and the degree to which finance was a phase of nearly every significant administrative, judicial, and military activity, combined to build their prestige and power. The traditions thus begun continue to affect French administration in the twentieth century.

The Chamber's basic function was verification of accounts. Five-sixths of this work concerned the accounts of field officials, and only the remaining sixth the accounts of the king's and other royal households, war treasurers, coinage mints, and managers of waters and forests. Even as acquisition of a room, a *chambre,* at the Palace had served to change a "committee" into a "chamber", the brown woolen cloth, *la bure,* covering the table on which the bailiffs laid their records of receipts and expenditures, gave the room with the table the name of *bureau.*

The Chamber symbolized its interposition between king and bailiff exactly as did the Parlement. That is, the newly designated bailiff took an oath before the Chamber of Accounts (as well as before the Parlement), and edicts of the king had to be registered by the Chamber before the financial aspects of their provisions could be assured of execution ...

The bailiffs, then, were subjected to multiple supervision. For appointment and assignment they depended on the king and his advisers, with the Great Council and the Chancery the key institutions of influence. For their judicial function they were subject to oversight by the Parlement, before which they took an oath, whose registration determined the enforceability of royal edicts, which heard appeals from the bailiffs' assizes and suits against the bailiffs, and whose central staff might direct the bailiffs to conduct local investigations or whose central staff members might themselves appear in the bailiwick. The bailiffs' financial functions, both getting and spending, were under the close scrutiny of the Chamber of Accounts, which, like the Parlement, exacted an oath from the bailiffs, registered royal decisions, and, in its own right, demanded a personal accounting by the bailiffs.

Note

1. The Knights Templar were a religious order of knights concerned mainly with defending the European crusader states in Syria. Inside Europe they engaged in banking and were believed to have great wealth. The order was destroyed under the attacks of Philip IV of France in the early fourteenth century [Ed.].

Chapter 12 THE LAWYERS OF LANGUEDOC IN LOCAL GOVERNMENT

JAN ROGOZINSKI (b. 1941) is a young American scholar who has specialized in the study of the lawyer class and social structure of lower Languedoc. He has argued that the royal government in the thirteenth and early fourteenth centuries relied far more heavily on the services of local gentry and burgesses than was formerly believed. This selection is from an article that deals with one aspect of this question—recruitment of subordinate judicial officers in the Beaucaire district.

One of the great southern provinces, the *sénéchaussée* of Nîmes was also the home of the University of Montpellier, at which Guillaume de Nogaret[1] and several other of the most notorious advisers of Philip the Fair received their legal training. During the reign of Saint Louis and of his grandson, the provincial administration was virtually autonomous and was seldom interfered with by the central government. While the seneschals themselves were northern French knights, their most important counsellors and officers were always lawyers belonging to the country gentry or urban patriciates of the *sénéchaussée*.[2] After 1328, the chief officials were, instead, northern clerks appointed directly from Paris. Local legists remained very influential, however, as members of an advisory council consulted by the administration in all matters seriously affecting the government of the province.

From Jan Rogozinski, "The Counsellors of the Seneschal of Beaucaire and Nîmes, 1250-1350," *Speculum*, XLIV (1969), pp. 421-423, 425-428, 432-433, 438-439. Reprinted by permission of the author and the Mediaeval Academy of America. Most of the author's footnotes are omitted.

Responsibility for the government of the *sénéchaussée* was vested in a single seneschal, appointed directly by the king and acting as his deputy. The seneschal represented the judicial powers of the crown, received homages, infeudated property, supervised the collection of royal rights, and summoned the militia of the towns and the nobility to war. Royal *enquêteurs*[3] and the Parlement of Paris could and occasionally did overrule the seneschal; he was, however, in sole control of day-to-day government, being assisted by various lesser officials to whom he delegated authority. Certain of these lesser officials (castellans, *viguiers,* and judges) represented the royal power in the localities; others (the *judex major, advocatus* and *procuratores regis,* and various lieutenants) aided the seneschal in the capital city of Nîmes and were present at meetings of his curia. During the reign of Philip of Valois [Philip VI], these officials became part of a formal hierarchy, the duties and powers of each more sharply defined. Ordinary administration of the *sénéchaussée* was entrusted to the highest officers, who were now appointed by the crown rather than by the seneschal. The seneschal himself became increasingly responsible for the military defense of the Midi under the command of a new officer, the royal lieutenant in Languedoc; but he still retained final judicial and administrative authority. The origins and experience of the seneschals thus greatly influenced the evolution of government in the *sénéchaussée.*

The first seneschals seem to have misused their extensive authority to enrich themselves and their families. Arbitrary and illegal acts were discovered by the *enquêteurs* of Saint Louis, who accordingly decreed ordonnances of reform in 1254. These ordonnances restored certain rights and required the seneschal to consult with the inhabitants of the province. The crown particularly sought to prevent the repetition of these abuses by requiring the frequent replacement of the seneschal, who was no longer permitted to acquire personal power by long tenure in any one office. After 1254, the seneschals were normally drawn from the minor nobility of the Orléanais or the Île-de-France. Essentially soldiers and administrators, they were transferred every two or three years from one *sénéchaussée to* another, usually receiving only southern posts despite their northern origins. Although the seneschal's assistants who possessed special training in law or finance were sometimes promoted to high offices in the central administration, the seneschal himself rarely rose above the rank of provincial governor.

In sum, the Capetian seneschals apparently satisfied the crown as administrators and military leaders, since several were posted to one *sénéchaussée* after another for many years. They were almost always, however, foreign to the Midi and without any knowledge of its laws and customs, which differed greatly from those of northern France. Roman law had been long recognized as the "custom" of southern France, and the *sénéchaussée.* As we have seen, the seschals prior to 1340 did not willing to pay high fees to retain *legum professores* from the University of Montpellier or even Bologna. The seneschal was the highest court of appeal in all civil cases, responsible to Parlement for the administration of justice throughout the entire *sénéchaussée*. As we have seen, the seneschals prior to 1340 did not possess any legal training, yet they were constantly required to review cases requiring a profound knowledge of Roman and Languedocian law regulating property and other rights. The seneschals appointed by Philip of Valois were of higher rank and experience, and one or two had some legal training; they were, however, primarily concerned with the military defense of the south and had little time left for their normal duties in the province.

How, then did these northern captains succeed for a century as governors of the *sénéchaussées* to which they were posted? At least part of their success, and perhaps the major part, resulted from the consistent use of southern advisers. The necessity of counsel with the governed was a commonplace of mediaeval political theory, emphasized by feudal, Roman, and canon law, as well as by scholastic learning. The Capetians expected the seneschal to administer the *sénéchaussée* in accordance with its *consuetudines approbatas*,[4] and royal ordonnances specifically required consultation with its inhabitants in matters affecting their welfare, such as the regulation of grain exports. The seneschals met these requirements; indeed, they went far beyond their letter. Large assemblies were frequently held to obtain the expert advice of jurists and notables and perhaps also to test and manipulate public opinion. Moreover, the seneschals also consistently sought the assistance of local legists in the routine administration of the *sénéchaussée* and turned to a small group of advisers whose loyalty to themselves and their predecessors had been obtained by appointment to lucrative offices or by other means.

Both the large meetings and those of the seneschal's personal advisers were sometimes called councils in the thirteenth and early fourteenth centuries. The word *consilium* was not yet tied to any specific institution; indeed, *consilium* was most frequently used as a common noun, serving roughly as a synonym for advice received from any group. It was used to designate the advice of the royal officers at meetings of the seneschal's curia; it was also used to describe the opinions of the royal judges and local notables at the assizes of the seneschal and the discussions of proposed legislation at meetings of men and the three estates of the *sénéchaussée*. Beginning in the late 1320's and early 1330's, as we shall see, *consilium* also took on an additional and more precise meaning, referring in particular to the "council of the *sénéchausée* composed of the counsellors belonging to the patriciate of Nîmes.

The most common form of consultative assembly was always the assizes. Meetings of the assizes were held at least twice each year at Nîmes and at major towns, such as Alès and Uzès, from which access to the capital was relatively difficult. At these meetings, the seneschal judged and legislated with the assistance of his major judge and a varying number of other royal judges and officials ...

The seneschals judged or legislated in important matters only after taking counsel in large gatherings. The solution of problems requiring immediate attention could not, however, await such assemblies, and the seneschal turned instead to a smaller body of advisers regularly present at the royal curia in Nîmes. These counsellors were generally professionally trained jurists resident in the *sénéchaussée* and many belonged to the local nobility or bourgeoisie. Like the larger consultative assemblies, this small group of advisers thus provided the seneschal with the advice and assistance of members of the ruling classes; during the reigns of the last Capetians, many of its members also served as high officials of the royal government in the *sénéchaussée* . . .

The seneschals of the later thirteenth century thus governed with the aid of southern legists, depending heavily upon the legal eminence of their counsellors and officers and also undoubtedly profiting from their long administrative experience and connections with the ruling classes. The continuity of administration provided by the long service of many of the legists must have been of particular value to the northern knights, who so briefly held office as seneschals. Several officials were replaced and new advisers were introduced by a number of seneschals as they entered into office, most noticeably in 1290, 1304, and 1311, and to a lesser extent in 1293. Normally, however, the seneschals continued to draw upon the knowledge of law and governmental procedure of the staff appointed by their predecessors. Most likely to be retained were the *advocati* and even more so the *procuratores regis,* whose positions were more administrative and less judicial (and thus political) than that of the *judex major.* During the reign of Philip the Fair, for example, three *procuratores* and one *advocatus* retained their positions for ten to twenty years under as many as five different seneschals.

Despite the apparent advantages of employing local legists, the seneschals lost the right to appoint their most important subordinates in the 1320's. During the reign of Philip VI, the *judices majores, advocati,* and *procuratores* were invariably northern French clerks named by royal letters of commission. The reasons for this change are unclear. Perhaps the appointment of northern officials to southern offices resulted from a desire for new sources of patronage. Also, the government of Philip of Valois may have resolved that the crown should no longer be despoiled by its staff, as it had been during the Capetian era . . .

Whatever the reasoning behind the policies of the Paris government, the administration in the *sénéchaussée* still required the assistance of local jurists and simply employed them under a new guise. As we have seen, one cannot speak of an advisory council distinct from the corps of officers during the reign of Philip the Fair. Half a century later, however, a special council did exist, its membership including not only the royal officers, but also twenty lawyers belonging to the patriciate of Nîmes. By the late 1330's it had become customary to consult in all important matters with this permanent and specific body of counsellors as well as with the royal officers and those whose interests were touched. When the seneschal issued a sentence at the assizes of Aiguesmortes in October 1322, he still "had counsel" solely with his officers and with landowners and legists resident in Aiguesmortes. Before issuing a sentence in a similar matter in 1339, the lieutenant of the seneschal noted that he had acted only after many meetings with the *consilium senescallie* and in the immediate presence of the royal officers and *consiliarii.*

Like the officers of the later thirteenth century, these *consiliarii* were lay lawyers of high social rank. Rather than being drawn from throughout the *sénéchaussée,* however, they were all inhabitants or citizens of Nîmes, and their residence in the capital enabled them to serve for years without holding a formal office. The existence of a body of legists who acted solely as advisers led contemporaries to speak of its members as *consiliarii* and to reserve the title of *consilium* particularly for those meetings attended by both the counsellors and the officers.

Under the Valois, as under the Capetians, the royal administration . . . consistently employed the services of southern lawyers, some of whom sought their own interests with as much zeal as those of the crown. The institutional forms changed in the fourteenth century because of the conflict between the need for counsellors and administrators cognizant of the laws and circumstances of the area and the crown's desire to control its representatives. After the defeat of the House of Toulouse, which had been too loosely bound by the tie of vassalage, Saint Louis neither infeudated the Midi to a great prince nor appointed a viceroy who might become autonomous. Instead, governmental power was entrusted to seneschals chosen from the minor nobility of the royal domain and changed constantly to prevent their forging new ties in the south. This very policy, however, when combined with Capetian respect for regional rights, virtually required the seneschal to consult with Languedocian nobles and legists and to secure the loyal advice of the most capable by appointment to high office.

The capability of these officers is unquestioned; they often served for many years, and several were asked to join the central administration in Paris. The government of Philip VI, nevertheless, removed this source of patronage from the senechal's control by appointing northern clerks to offices in the *sénéchaussée'* Despite this decision, the administration remained dependent upon local lawyers. The royal officers wished to attach permanently to the government knowledgeable and influential residents of the province, and added to their number at meetings of the court of the *sénéchaussée* a group of lawyers belonging to the patriciate of Nîmes. A specific advisory council thus came into existence in the 1330s, precisely because the royal officers were no longer themselves drawn from the *sénéchaussée* . . . Whether or not the crown approved, the intellectual skills of these legists made their cooperation desirable and thus enabled them to acquire new authority, wealth, and even personal nobility.

Notes

1. Guillaume de Nogaret, an influential councillor of Philip IV, led the expedition that abducted Pope Boniface VIII in 1303 as a consequence of his bitter quarrel with the king [Ed.].
2. "Country gentry" signifies families possessing both personal nobility and sufficient rural property to bring them privilege and power in the locality in which they lived, although their

holdings were insignificant in comparison to those of the territorial princes or the titled peerage. By "urban patriciate" is meant the small group of families, both noble and nonnoble, who controlled the government of their community because of their wealth and social status and through the use of electoral chicanery.

3. *Enquêteurs* (sometimes also called *réformateurs*) were commissioners of inquiry sent out by the king, beginning in the reign of Saint Louis, to hear complaints against royal officials. To this initial role as a kind of *ombudsman*, Philip IV and his successors added other functions, often using *enquêteurs* to find additional sources of revenue [Ed].

4. Literally, "approved customs," meaning the accepted legal traditions of the district [Ed.].

Chapter 13 THE ROLE OF LAWYERS IN THE CENTRAL GOVERNMENT

FRANKLIN J. PEGUES (b. 1924), a professor of history at Ohio State University, has specialized in the study of the civil servants and the universities of the thirteenth and fourteenth centuries. Where Rogozinski concentrated on the lawyers of a particular region, the book from which this selection is taken deals with prominent lawyers from all parts of France who were employed by the central government during the period 1285-1328. Pegues attacks the older view that these men were largely of bourgeois origin and hostile to the nobility.

How did Thierry, Guizot, and Michelet[1] view the lawyers of the last Capetians? They saw them as the unalterable opponents of noble privilege, the legal architects of an undivided public authority, and as men who laid the cornerstone of an egalitarian society. The lawyers played the role of revolutionaries, and it is needless to comment further on the fact that the view of these three historians was determined by the issues of the French Revolution. The essence of the interpretation was contained in the thesis of a struggle between the baron and the legist, and the baron represented both the lay and ecclesiastical nobility. But even Guizot warned against the unqualified acceptance of this thesis for he saw in the events of 1315 the use of baronial lawyers to prosecute royal lawyers. There is more to it than that, however, for in the face of historical evidence the thesis must be completely

From Franklin J. Pegues, *The Lawyers of the Last Capetians* (copyright © 1962 by Princeton University Press), pp. 221-228. Reprinted by permission of Princeton University Press.

rejected. Every noble, great or small, and every ecclesiastical house, episcopal or monastic, had an entourage of legal counselors who served them well and faithfully because they were dependent upon their employers for economic reward. The lawyers were not interested in betraying or destroying their noble clients but in extracting from them as much compensation as possible.

The thesis of the struggle between baron and legist supposes, moreover, that a particular group of lawyers served only the king and served him with singleness of purpose ... The lawyers undoubtedly counted the king as the most important of their employers for he was the greatest of the nobles and offered far greater compensation. But they enjoyed the custom and presumably the right to serve other clients while engaged in the royal service, and this custom remained as prevalent under the Valois kings as it had been under the Capetians.

A graver aspect of the conjectured struggle of the legist against the baron is that it proposes the unmistakable concept of a class struggle in fourteenth-century France, and more especially a class struggle between the nobility on the one hand and the lawyers as representatives of the middle class on the other ... More of the lawyers were noble than middle class and, on the sheer weight of numbers, the idea of a class struggle between the middle class lawyers and the feudal barons will not hold up. There may have been a class struggle in fourteenth-century France, but it most assuredly was not waged by the lawyers against the nobles.

To say that there was no class struggle is not to say that lawyers of middle class origin had no class consciousness. But it was the variety of class consciousness which made them wish to achieve the status of the most socially approved class. We therefore come to the aspirations of the lawyers. If we draw conclusions from what we know of their behavior, we must say that they wanted first of all status and approval, and the first step toward this goal was the acquisition of wealth in land or money. It sometimes appeared that they did not wish to be ennobled but rather to have the wealth and social approval that the nobles enjoyed ....

What does a study of the Capetian lawyers reveal about the nature of Philip the Fair's reign? Their behavior and the work which they accomplished indicated that neither they nor Philip were engaged in a conscious drive toward political absolutism. Philip the Fair was not a power-mad monarch and certainly not a political despot. Everything about his reign points to him as a needy king. He was caught in the grip of the inflationary trend which had come out of the thirteenth century and, ultimately, out of the economic revolution that had occurred in the eleventh and twelfth centuries. His ordinances, his legislation and his commissions scarcely mention the ideal of political absolutism. But they constantly refer to the inflated cost of living and they constantly assert, not his right to legislate for all of France, but his need to tax as widely as possible. Beyond the matter of ordinary taxation, they give evidence of his desperate need for extraordinary sources of income. This we take to be the sense of Philip the Fair's reign and of the work done by his lawyers. Historians know well that the struggle with Boniface[2] was born of the issue of taxation. The Templars[3] constituted no internal threat to the king's political rule, but they did control an enormous depository of wealth. The alterations of currency and the confiscation of Jewish and Lombard property are too transparent for comment. Far from being the architects and agents of monarchical absolutism, the lawyers advised the king on the acquisition of income, formulated his taxation policy, and then went into the field where they became the agents and executors of a fiscal absolutism.

This fiscal absolutism was one of the lawyers' contributions to the French monarchy. The political position of a Francis I or of a Louis XIV was made possible in part by the early growth of this fiscal absolutism. In the hands of Nogaret, Villepreux, and Latilly,[4] this absolutism sometimes deteriorated into fiscal terrorism. Even at this point, primarily political objectives seemed to be absent. It is true that Philip the Fair issued ordinances in which he repeatedly prohibited the judicial duel, private wars, and tournaments among the nobles. Even here, he usually made it clear that the prohibition applied only when the kingdom was at war. The Baronial Revolt of 1314 arose not so much from the expansion of royal jurisdiction at the expense of seigneurial jurisdiction, but rather from the too frequent subsidies, the incessant alterations of money, and the intolerable behavior of some of the king's favorites. Pierre de Latilly was interested in collecting money in 1297, not in proclaiming or extending royal sovereignty. His heavy hand fell on the common people and scarcely ever on the nobles. There was the constant and natural tendency for nobles and others to encroach on royal rights, and the numerous commissions sent out by Philip the Fair, the commissions on nonnoble acquisitions of noble lands, on money, on servile dues, on the "reformation" of various districts, were directed more to the reestablishment of ancient royal rights than to the creation of new ones. In the execution of these commissions, the lawyers and other agents sometimes gave the appearance of extending royal jurisdiction. The essence of Philip's fiscal absolutism lay in his constant and often cruel drive to re-establish, to expand, and ultimately to nationalize, all of the possible sources of royal revenue.

Notes

1. Thierry, Guizot, and Michelet were perhaps the three greatest French historians of the early and middle nineteenth century. They established many of the traditions of modern French historiography [Ed.].

2. Pope Boniface VIII (1294-1303), whose bitter conflict with Philip IV was perhaps the most famous occurrence of the king's eventful reign [Ed.].

3. See note 1 in the Fesler selection in Part IV for a description of the Knights Templar [Ed.].

4. Three of Philip IV's most active and powerful lawyers [Ed.].

Part Four: THE ENIGMA OF PHILIP THE FAIR

Chapter 14 PHILIP IV: A KING WHO WAS CONSTITUTIONAL

JOSEPH R. STRAYER (b. 1904), Dayton-Stockton Professor of History at Princeton University, is one of the most distinguished medieval historians in the United States. His scholarly studies deal extensively with feudalism and with the administrative history of England and France in the thirteenth and fourteenth centuries. This selection, taken from one of Strayer's many articles on the government of Philip IV illustrates his conviction that Philip did control basic policy himself. It shows why Strayer believes Philip was a "constitutionall" monarch.

The reign of Philip the Fair offers one of the great paradoxes of French history. One the one hand, it sees the culmination of the medieval French monarchy; the royal government reaches a peak of power which it is not to attain again for generations. On the other hand, the king who presides over the government during these crowded years of great events is a shadowy, elusive figure, almost completely hidden behind a screen of bureaucrats. It is hard to prove that any important act of the reign was the result of a personal decision by the king. It is easy to argue that he did nothing, and by doing nothing allowed his ministers to express the traditions of the bureaucracy in a relentless drive for power. And yet those who believe that the important decisions of the reign were made by Philip's ministers merely change the form but not the substance of the paradox. For no one minister held power

From Joseph R. Strayer, "Philip the Fair—a Constitutional King," *American Historical Review*, LXII (1956-1957), pp. 18-26, 29-32. Reprinted, with footnotes omitted, by permission of the author.

throughout the reign and no one minister had complete control of the government for even a short period. Yet basic policy remained constant, though tactics changed. If the king did not give continuity and direction to policy, who did? Can it be true that the whole bureaucracy was so imbued with the spirit of aggrandizement that it made no difference who was selected to sit in the royal Council? Or did Philip express his hidden desires through a careful choice of ministers?

This problem worried Philip's contemporaries, and it has worried historians ever since. On the whole, French writers of the early fourteenth century tended to believe that Philip was dominated by evil counsellors ... Bishop Bernard Saisset[1] made many indiscreet remarks, but the one which stung most and has been remembered longest was his comparison of Philip to the owl: "the handsomest of birds which is worth absolutely nothing ... such is our king of France who is the handsomest man in the world and who can do nothing except to stare at men." Foreign chroniclers such as the Italian Villani and the Fleming Gilles le Muisis also believed that Philip was a figurehead. Even Boniface VIII, in listing Philip's offenses ... thought it wise to insert some lines attacking the king's evil counsellors, though he added that this was no excuse and that the king bore full responsibility for allowing such men to have power. The Aragonese writer who said that Philip was a masterful ruler, emperor, pope, and king rolled into one, was an exception.

Modern historians have been less willing to write Philip off as a nonentity. The Germans, who see Philip as the originator of the French drive to the east, are especially emphatic on this point ... [They all] agree that Philip gave consistency and strength to French policy during his reign. The English historian Boase warns against "believing that so much of France was created ... with no central guiding will." French scholars, who should know the facts best, are a little less sure. Boutaric believed in Philip's leadership and personal responsiblity, but Boutaric wrote at the very beginning of serious scholarly investigation of the period. Langlois felt that the problem was insoluble, but his discussion does not do much to convince the reader that Philip was a strong king. Digard, without taking a very definite stand, tended to ascribe responsibility to the "counsellors of the king," to the "court," to Pierre Flote,[2] rather than to Philip. On the other hand Fawtier, who knows the documents of the reign better than any other historian, has no doubt that Philip controlled and directed his government. He admits that some measures may have been initiated by members of the Council rather than by the king, but he is sure that Philip always knew and approved what was done in his name ...

We can begin by admitting that many things were done in the king's name about which he knew nothing. France was a large country and had, even then, an unusually high density of bureaucrats, both at Paris and in the provinces. Most of these bureaucrats were trying to distinguish themselves by ceaseless activity in preserving, discovering, and increasing royal rights and revenues. Within certain limits, they had a free hand; they did not have to go to the king for authority for each act, and they received few specific orders regarding their ordinary work.

Yet there were limits, and these limits became apparent whenever a provincial official tried to go too far or too fast in his task of increasing royal power. The government of Philip the Fair was not very tender of the rights of bishops or of communes, but it had more respect for these rights than many local officials. It preferred to hold at least to the letter of the law; it would rather restrict than abolish privileges. It also knew that certain bishops were influential enough to need careful handling and that the loyalty of certain provinces (especially in the South) was too uncertain to stand much rough treatment. Therefore we have dozens of letters forbidding royal officials to trouble bishops such as Guillaume le Maire of Angers, or communes such as that of Toulouse. Some of these letters are so emphatic and so personal that it is hard to believe that anyone could have written them except the king himself . . .

It is, of course, impossible to prove conclusively that these letters were written by direct order of the king. But it is clear that there was an inner circle in the government which had full control over all other royal officials and which insisted that its policies should be carried out at all levels of administration. The character of Philip's reign was not determined by a blind drive for power by a horde of petty bureaucrats. Policy was made at the highest level by a very few men, by the king and his Council.

Accepting this, one can still argue that the king was the least important member of the governing group, that he merely ratified decisions which were made by the Council as a whole, or by some of its leading members. This hypothesis would seem to be strengthened, at first glance, by evidence that the king did not always know what members of the Council did in his name. From time to time we hear of letters which have been obtained surreptitiously, of conflicting promises made by the king and members of the Council, of contradictory royal charters. But if these documents prove that the king did not always remember his promises or that he was not always informed of what was done in his name, they also prove that no one else was in complete control. In the competition for royal favors several men in succession might gain the king's ear; there was no single all-powerful favorite through whom patronage was channeled. Even more important, we hear of these contradictory orders because the king, in the long run, did become aware that his wishes were not being observed. And in every case he had his way; the surreptitious or conflicting letters were revoked; the claimant to whom the king really wished to give income or office received it. The only safe conclusion from this evidence is that there was some inefficiency, some failure of communication in the French government of the late thirteenth century. The same weaknesses are apparent in any other medieval government; they are not entirely absent in much more highly organized modern states.

Furthermore, someone in the government—almost certainly the king or the keeper of the seal—made an effort to prevent the appearance of these unauthorized or conflicting letters. The rule was gradually established thatevery document issued in the king's name must carry at the bottom the name of the notary who wrote it and the name of the official who ordered it written. The earliest examples of this practice which I have found come from the 1290s; by 1314 most documents are so authenticated. What is even more helpful to the historian is that the scribes who copied royal letters into the registers of the last years of the reign included in their copies the names of the notaries, and of the officials who ordered the letters written. This means that we have hundreds of cases in which we know precisely who took the responsibility for a certain act of government.

Most of the documents which appear in the registers deal only with trivial matters—such things as amortizations, approval of farms made by local officials, exchanges of property, gifts, acts of pardon and of grace. This has its advantages. We can be sure that we are watching the normal operations of government, not extraordinary procedures invented for great occasions. And it is at least a reasonable supposition that the men who work steadily on these routine matters will be well informed about the kingdom, well versed in administrative procedures, well acquainted with all important members of the court, and hence influential in making major decisions.

A rough tabulation of the names on these documents during the last five years of the reign yields interesting results. First of all, a rather large number of men—at least thirty-two—have authority to order letters written in the king's name. Not all of these men are very active; the great lords of the Council, men such as the counts of Valois and St. Pol, seldom command letters. On the other hand, there are about fifteen names which appear again and again. Purely numerical comparisons among this group would be meaningless, since the record is incomplete, and some letters are more important than others. It is clear, however, that there is a certain amount of specialization. For example, Philippe le Convers orders most of the letters dealing with forests; Hugues de la Celle is the expert on the Saintonge-Poitou area; Guillaume de Marcilly and Guillaume Cocatrix have been given the task of buying lands and houses to make room for the extension of the royal palace. Others seem to have more general interests; in this group Nogaret, as keeper of the seal, and Marigny, as financial expert, are conspicuous but not unique. They are no busier than some of their colleagues and they have no exclusive powers; for example, Marigny is far from being the only councillor to deal with financial matters. Neither Nogaret nor Marigny is in the position of a chief minister; there is no chain of command which passes through them. They are merely two of a group of fifteen or so men who are very busy writing letters in the king's name. If there is any direction to this activity at all, it must come either from the group as a whole (and it seems a little large to act as a unit), or from the king.

This leads to the most surprising fact of all. Out of a sample of 658 documents taken from registers JJ45 through JJ50, 280 bear the notation "per dominum regem." That is, over two-fifths of a very ordinary batch of letters were ordered by the king in person. In many cases there seems to be no very good reason for the king to take a personal interest, and it is impossible to establish categories of letters which were warranted by the king alone . . .

To sum up, the impression given by this material is that the king controlled and directed the routine work of the government. He was the one who assigned tasks to his councillors, and he reserved the right to act directly and personally in any matter which interested him. There were too many councillors, and responsibility was too evenly divided among them, for any single minister to dominate the government. At the very least, the king was busier than any member of his Council; he was informed about a great variety of matters and he made many decisions. Certainly Philip was not the lazy king who, according to some chroniclers, did nothing but hunt, nor yet the stupid king described by Bernard Saisset who understood nothing and only stared at people.

This king who took such interest in the small details of government cannot have been indifferent to greater affairs. If no one councillor was given full responsibility for handling routine business, it is a little difficult to believe that any councillor had unlimited power in making important decisions . . . The basic policies of the reign appear quite early, long before famous ministers such as Flote or Nogaret or Marigny play any role in the central government. For example, pressure by royal officials on the Church increased sharply in the first years of the reign; by 1291 Nicholas IV could say that the churches of France were complaining daily of grave injuries. Attempts to annex imperial territories were also well under way by the early 1290s, and the *parlement* was already intervening in the affairs of Gascony and of Flanders. Even more significant is the fact that members of the royal family played an essential role in Philip's foreign policy. Franche-Comté was to be annexed through a carefully planned series of marriages of French princes; English friendship was to be gained by the union of Philip's daughter and Edward [I]'s son; Germany was to be controlled by proposing a French prince as a candidate for the imperial throne. Anyone who has read the documents of the reign knows that Philip took a deep personal interest in all matters touching members of his family, and it is inconceivable that he could have allowed his children and his brothers to be used as pawns to support a policy devised by others. He undoubtedly took advice, but the final decision on royal marriages and candidacies for foreign thrones must have been his alone. And yet such marriages and candidacies, as we have seen, were essential elements of French policy . . .

This long discussion has still not resolved the contradiction with which the paper began. On the one hand, there is too much evidence that Philip took an active part in both small and great affairs to write him down as a figurehead. On the other hand, it is clear that both individual ministers and the Council as a whole had too much power and responsibility to be dismissed as rubber stamps. And the king's habit of letting his ministers speak for him on the most important occasions cannot be explained as just a political trick; it seems to have expressed a deep-seated conviction that this was the proper way to act.

The contradiction can be resolved only if we remember a fact which Philip's contemporaries never let him forget: that he was the grandson of St. Louis. He had grown up in a court which was saturated with memories of the holy king; he had worked hard to secure the canonization of his grandfather; it was only natural that he should seek to imitate this model monarch. This meant, first of all, piety, and few historians have ever doubted that Philip was honestly and sincerely pious. But with the piety went a deep sense of the dignity, the greatness, and the mission of French kingship. The king was the high priest of the "religion of monarchy," remote, aloof, withdrawn from all vulgar quarrels. He was to be approached only through his acolytes; the sacred mysteries were not to be revealed to the profane. Finally, a good king did not govern arbitrarily; he did not act on his own whims or make decisions in haste. He must be surrounded by "prud'hommes" who advised and informed him; he must always take counsel before acting. St. Louis had felt that even in the midst of a battle he must hold a council before changing his plans. Philip the Fair acted the same way in the midst of his political battles. But no one has ever doubted that St. Louis made his own decisions after asking for advice, and there is no reason to suppose that Philip was any more bound by the opinions of his Council.

The best phrase to describe Philip is somewhat anachronistic; he wanted to be a "constitutional" king. But if we give the word "constitutional" its broadest meaning it is a fair description of his policy. Philip tried to conform to the traditions of the French monarchy and the practices of the French government. As far as possible, he governed his realm through a well-established system of courts and administrative officials. He always asked the advice of responsible men; he was influenced by that advice in working out the details of his general policy. He tried to stay at least within the letter of the law; he tried to observe the customs of the kingdom. When he had to go beyond established custom he always sought to justify his action and to obtain the consent of those who were affected . . . At the very least, consent satisfied the king's desire to remain within the limits of legality. Often, of course, it had important political consequences as well; it certainly facilitated the collection of taxes and strengthened the monarchy in the struggle with Boniface VIII.

If we think of Philip as a "constitutional" king we see why he preferred to work through his ministers and Council. This was the proper and customary way to act; it showed that the king was taking the advice of men learned in precedents and in the law. It preserved the king as a symbol of unity, far above transitory disputes and petty considerations of gain or loss. But it does not mean that Philip refused responsibility and allowed others to govern in his name. He worked hard at his job of being a king; he knew what was going on in his kingdom, and no important act could be accomplished until he made the final decision . . .

In fact, Philip's relations with his Council were not unlike those of a modern prime minister with his cabinet. Special tasks were assigned to each member, advice was always asked and often taken, but final decision and general direction of policy remained with the king. This relationship made it easy for Philip to be a "constitutional" king. He could allow his officials to act in his name because he knew that they would serve his purposes ...

Notes

1. Bernard Saisset, bishop of Pamiers and an enemy of the king, was a key figure in the royal struggle with Boniface VIII [Ed.].

2. Another key figure in the struggle with Boniface, Flote was an influential royal adviser who headed the chancery until his death in 1302 [Ed.].

Chapter 15 PHILIP IV: A KING WHO AVOIDED BEING CONSTITUTIONAL

BRYCE LYON (b. 1920), professor of history at Brown University, is primarily a student of English medieval history, but he has been active in the developing field of comparative institutions, studying government and finance on both sides of the Channel. He defines medieval constitutionalism as a balance of power between monarchs and other political forces. In the following selection he criticizes Strayer's conception of constiutionality and denies that Philip IV can properly be called a constitutional king.

One seems justified in asking why it has recently become fashionable to regard Philip the Fair as a "constitutional king." If English historians are agreed that Edward was a "sort" of constitutional king,[1] how, given the disparity in power, could Philip have also been a constitutional king? It is conceivable that he was constitutional, though less so than Edward, and that the French criteria for a king's being constitutional differed from the English, but what one really wants to know is what made a medieval king constitutional.

If in the thoughtful and provocative article of ... J. R. Strayer, published a few years ago [see preceding selection], one follows the shifting opinion of historians

From Bryce D. Lyon, "What Made a Medieval Monarch Constitutional?" in *Essays in Medieval History Presented to Bertie Wilkinson*, edited by T. A. Sandquist and M. R. Powicke (Copyright Canada 1969 by University of Toronto Press), pp. 158-161, 169-175. Reprinted by permission of the author and the University of Toronto Press.

on the nature of Philip the Fair's power, he discovers that until twenty-five years ago it was generally agreed that Philip was an illusive, shady character whose intentions and objectives were concealed by the efficient, ambitious councillors and servants who surrounded him and who initiated and implemented royal policy. The prevailing view was that Philip was not an attractive or reliable person, that he was ineffective and quiescent in government, and that the tremendous power achieved by the Capetian monarchy during his reign stemmed mostly from his capable ministers.

Robert Fawtier challenged this interpretation, asserting that Philip dominated his government and was active in its work, that he was responsible for the achievements of his reign. The Fawtier position gained the support of Professor Strayer who investigated the performance of Philip by looking at him through administrative and legal records of the central government rather than through the eyes of contemporary chroniclers. Professor Strayer concluded that Philip "controlled and directed the routine work of the government. He was the one who assigned tasks to his councillors, and he reserved the right to act directly and personally in any matter which interested him . . . At the very least, the king was busier than any member of his Council." Furthermore, Philip not only concerned himself with the "small details" but was involved in the "greater affairs." He was responsible for the struggle against Boniface VIII, the affair of the Templars, and diplomatic and political moves involving an important range of subjects. Philip was no figurehead!

In the last part of his study Professor Strayer portrays Philip as a constitutional king. His thesis is that Philip behaved in a constitutional manner because he conformed to the traditions and practices of French government, observed the customs and laws of the realm, obtained consent from those concerned when he went beyond normal practices or the law, worked through established legal procedures and courts, and invariably asked for the advice of his council. Though acknowledging that ultimately Philip controlled all, Professor Strayer contends that because Philip stayed within the letter of the law and took counsel he was a constitutional king.

While Professor Strayer has reinforced Fawtier's position that Philip the Fair was an active and powerful king, in portraying him as a constitutional king he has parted from Fawtier who saw no effective control exercised over his power. Fawtier's last words on the question were that in the kingdom of France there was no control over the king and that although kings might consult with their councils they were never bound by the advice received. Even the assemblies of estates convened by Philip wielded no control . . . .The problem can only be clarified, it seems, by comparing what Philip did and was able to do with what Edward I did and was able to do. Essentially the problem reduces itself to the practical consideration of what each king could "get away with." Regardless of theory on limitation of royal power and regardless of the restrictive influence of law and custom, the "constitutionalism" of both kings was largely a matter of practical politics.

There is not enough evidence to support the generalization that a succession of ineffective, untalented, and inactive kings necessarily contributed to the rise of constitutional government, but it is a fact that weak kings were more easily controlled, and controlled by various political configurations, and that such control could lead to constitutional government. Although some French kings, such as Charles VI, were controlled by political factions of nobles and although, as dauphin, the future Charles V was temporarily restricted in the exercise of royal authority by Etienne Marcel and his followers in the estates[2] such control was transitory and led to no permanent limitation of royal power. In England, however, the undeniably weak reign of Henry III, as well as the reigns of Edward II, Richard II, and Henry VI, encouraged baronial control in the form of councils, control that led ultimately to constitutional government. It seems to follow, therefore, that active and able kings were controlled only with difficulty.

Concurring with Professor Strayer that Philip the Fair was an active king in control of his government, but doubting his "constitutionalism," let us now consider the activity and power of Edward I . . .

The evidence . . . supports the position that Edward was active in the routine and great affairs of the realm, that he was in control of them and of the men who counseled him and who exercised delegated authority. Edward has emerged as a probably more active king than Philip the Fair and one who exercised even more control over his government. In Edward, England had an ambitious, industrious, observant, keen, and practical king. But was such a strong king also constitutional, and are the arguments of Professor Strayer, depicting Philip the Fair as a constitutional king, valid also for Edward?

Philip the Fair, according to Professor Strayer, regarded his grandfather Saint Louis as the model of what a king ought to be. Philip therefore tried to be honest, pious, and dignified. Above all, he had a sense of the mission of French kingship and, as Robert Fawtier has expressed it, assumed the role of high priest of the "religion of monarchy." In some ways Edward resembled Philip. As a young man Edward had known Saint Louis and had admired his lofty concept of kingship. He agreed with Saint Louis that kingship was a high trust for which a king was responsible only to God, that kings could not be shorn of their rightful prerogatives by mortal men. But although he emulated the good qualities of Louis, and despite his high concept of royal power, it would be difficult to prove that Edward regarded himself as the high priest of the "religion of monarchy."

But what does this have to do with constitutionalism? History has shown that even virtuous kings who acknowledged responsibility only to God for their acts were not constitutional; they were, in fact, despotic. Although the medieval successors of Philip the Fair continued to share his admiration for Saint Louis and considered themselves pious Christians, the French monarchy did not emerge from the middle ages as a constitutional monarchy; it emerged as a very absolute one. Few are the historians who would defend the thesis that Richard II, James I, or

Louis XIV were constitutional kings because of their elevated concept of kingship or their admission of responsibility only to God. It simply does not follow that because Saint Louis was a good and just king who respected the rights of his people he was constitutional, or that because Philip the Fair and other kings admired Saint Louis and gave the impression of following in his footsteps they were constitutional.

Philip the Fair, Professor Strayer contends, followed the guidelines of his grandfather by conforming to the traditions of French monarchy, by governing through the existing system of courts and administrative officials, and by adhering to established law and custom. He managed, as Professor Strayer says, "to stay at least within the letter of the law." But cannot some of these conclusions be questioned? Did Philip work within the existing framework of administration, respect the law, and use established courts and judicial procedure? To be sure, he still used *enquêteurs*, but were they the same kind of official as Saint Louis used and were their instructions still to weed out bad government and corrupt officials and to remedy the grievances of subjects? Would Saint Louis have proceeded against the Knights Templars in the fashion that Philip did? In this celebrated struggle did Philip respect law and allow accepted procedure to be followed in the proper courts? These queries are perhaps best answered by Professor Strayer's phrase: "He tried to stay at least within the letter of the law." . . .

According to Professor Strayer, Philip the Fair, knowing that a good king never acted arbitrarily, always deliberated with his council before making decisions. This is not to say, however, that Philip had to take counsel or that he acted upon the counsel given. Professor Strayer is careful to emphasize that Philip was never bound by the advice of his council, that he made his own decisions, decisions often contrary to the counsel received. He controlled the council and "in the last analysis he controlled the government."

Though the relations of Edward with his council were much the same, there was a basic difference. Edward was wary of his council; he knew the embarrassment it could cause a king. He remembered that in 1215 the barons had tried to control John by means of a baron-dominated council. He knew from experience all the trouble councils had caused his father . . . Edward took advice from his council and used it much as did Philip the Fair. But, despite his control of the council, he distrusted it; it made him nervous. Could he not lose control of it? Could it not control him? Such thoughts never entered Philip's mind. Never had councils controlled his predecessors and never would they control him.

That Philip and Edward took counsel from their councils does not make them constitutional kings; both controlled their councils and both had the ultimate decision. But Edward had less control; he knew that at times his control was precarious and feared that it might be challenged. Though a strong king, Edward must have known that he was less powerful than Philip and that he had to scheme and struggle to retain control over his council and government. He lived under the shadow of a powerful baronage which could not be ignored, and he therefore had less freedom of action than Philip. Encounters of Edward and his predecessors with the baronage afforded dramatic proof that royal power was not absolute, that Edward's desires and objectives must take into account the desires and objectives of the barons. Neither Philip the Fair nor his predecessors had known such a limitation of their authority.

It is true, as Professor Strayer has stated, that when Philip the Fair embarked upon important projects or demanded extraordinary support and pecuniary contributions, he summoned large assemblies to Paris or consulted with local assemblies to obtain counsel, consent, and a wide consensus of support. Edward behaved similarly, but again with some important differences. He seldom dealt with local assemblies; usually, he summoned large assemblies increasingly composed of clergy, baronage, knights of the shires, and burgesses of the boroughs to give him counsel, consent, or support for weighty affairs of the realm. Edward was either unable or seldom tried to negotiate with regional assemblies; almost invariably he dealt with one large assembly-parliament which spoke more and more for the whole realm. Unlike Philip who only used his assemblies to obtain money, to propagandize his policies, or to gain support from his subjects, and who never felt compelled to grant or promise concessions in return for what he wanted and got, Edward had to negotiate with parliament ever more frequently and to make concessions in return for what he obtained. He realized that when he had to summon a parliament he would have to deal with it on a *quid pro quo* basis. On those occasions when he demanded service considered unjustified by custom, when he taxed arbitrarily and heavily, when he forcibly seized the goods of his subjects, or when he introduced unpopular innovations, he was backed into a corner and humbled by the confirmation of the Charters and the *Articuli super cartas.*[3]

For actions and demands far more arbitrary than Edward's, Philip the Fair suffered no such indignity. He was never humbled or forced to admit any definite restriction of his authority. Imagine what his reaction would have been to a restriction that henceforth on no account would he "take from our kingdom such aids, taxes, prises, except by the common assent of the whole kingdom and for the common benefit of the same kingdom, saving the ancient aids and prises due and accustomed"! After his death there was revulsion against what was considered an arbitrary reign and his sons were faced with regional leagues of nobles demanding concessions that would limit royal authority and return conditions to those known under Saint Louis. The outcome is well known. Philip's sons were able to delay and to negotiate, to isolate the leagues, and finally to reduce them to impotence. They emerged virtually unscathed and passed on their majestic power to their Valois successors. Not under Philip the Fair, not under his sons, and not under their successors of the fourteenth and fifteenth centuries was there any force or group of forces powerful and united enough to compel real and permanent limitation of royal authority.

What, then, made a medieval king constitutional? To call Philip the Fair a constitutional king because he gave the appearance of respecting tradition and law, took counsel from his council, and occasionally consulted with assemblies about extraordinary demands and problems is unrealistic. Although Philip did these things, he was not forced to do them; his control over council and assemblies was supreme. If he used established legal apparatus and administrative organs, he did so just within the letter of the law. Never did he have to work out his problems with a strong political bloc that had the power to make him govern according to defined principles of government. How he behaved was really his own affair, and so it was for most of his successors.

Edward welcomed limitation of his authority no more than Philip, but he had to govern his realm knowing that there were effective limitations. He had always to negotiate with a united and resourceful baronage. Increasingly this negotiation had to be in Parliament which, in addition to the baronage, came to include the clergy, knights, and burgesses. Despite his efforts to ignore these groups and to govern without their general approval, he could not; he had to acknowledge that on great affairs of the realm, such as taxation and fundamental legislation, Parliament held the trump cards. Edward was forced into being a constitutional king by political realities expressed in that institution known by the late thirteenth century as parliament. Because Philip the Fair never had to live with or make accommodation with these political realities, he never became a constitutional king. It was not theory, not professed belief in tradition and established institutions and law, not admiration of a saintly king, and not counsel from a council, but political pressure become constant and institutionalized that made medieval kings constitutional. To understand medieval constitutionalism otherwise is to misunderstand medieval politics.

Notes

1. Edward I (1272-1307) was one of the most able kings of medieval England and a slightly older contemporary of Philip IV of France. During his reign the English Parliament developed into an important institution [Ed.].

2. Etienne Marcel was a prominent merchant and official of the city of Paris, whose jealousy of certain high royal financial officers caused him to lead a rebellion against the monarchy during the captivity of John II, 1356-1358. He found allies in the Estates General, which met several times in those troubled years [Ed.].

3. These documents, issued under pressure by Edward I in the late 1290s, had the effect of reaffirming and elaborating upon certain traditional rights of the barons and people of England which restricted the king's freedom of action [Ed.].

Part Five DEVELOPING INSTITUTIONS OF GOVERNMENT

Chapter 16 PHILIP IV AND THE MORALITY OF TAXATION

ELIZABETH A. R. BROWN (b. 1932), a professor of history at Brooklyn College in New York, has specialized in the comparative fiscal history of England and France in the first quarter of the fourteenth century. She has written articles on several aspects of this subject, but perhaps her most original contribution to our understanding of the medieval French monarchy concerns the moral aspects of taxation, as taught by the legists and theologians and understood by the kings themselves. Her conclusions about Philip the Fair's attitude toward taxation have been set forth in several papers read at scholarly conferences. The selection printed here is a slightly revised excerpt from these papers.

Philip the Fair and his ministers were great experimenters and inventive politicians, and it was well that they were, for they had to deal with crises such as earlier kings had never faced, and the problems demanded original solutions... Philip had to gain the material as well as the moral support of his subjects. Moral backing was relatively easy to secure, for Philip had the propagandists, the authority, and the sanctions to be able to extract it. Perhaps even more important, moral support was eminently easy to give. Approval and endorsement cost nothing and involved no loss of property. Material support was quite a different matter, however, for it

From Elizabeth A. R. Brown, "Politics, Taxation and Discontent: Philip the Fair's Legacy to his Sons," unpublished paper originally read at a conference of the Society for French Historical Studies, Ann Arbor, 1966, with additional excerpts from a later version of this paper, "Conscience, Politics, and Taxation under Philip the Fair," read at a meeting of the Medieval Club of New York in December, 1966, and some further minor revisions made in 1970 by the author, with whose permission this selection is printed here.

required actual personal service or payment of money. To persuade subjects to undergo such deprivation required propaganda more compelling, sanctions more effective, and authority more impressive than was the case when only nominal endorsement was sought . . .

Historians have shown how adeptly Philip's lawyers and preachers developed the theoretical rights and duties of the monarchy, by expanding old claims and deriving novel rights from hallowed customs, maxims of Roman law, and biblical quotations. They have often tended to assume that the assertion of the king's right to override private privileges in emergencies implied his actual ability to do so, and have perceived a recognizable prototype of the modern sovereign state in the France of Philip the Fair; they have thought of the medieval French monarchy as attaining the height of its power under Philip's rule . . .

Since the middle of the twelfth century, theorists of all persuasions—students of Roman law, canon law, customary law—had assumed the right of kings to seek the material support of their subjects in cases of extraordinary need. As the thirteenth century progressed, the chorus grew louder and more articulate. In the early 1270s St. Thomas Aquinas had soothed the conscience of the duchess of Brabant by assuring her that the ruler was perfectly justified in taking extraordinary levies to provide for the common utility or maintain the honorable estate of the prince; he also said that if the ruler's revenues were insufficient for his ordinary needs, he might impose fixed taxes on his subjects. A little later, in the 1280s, Beaumanoir proclaimed that in case of war, the king might take measures for the common profit, and he believed that in such a case all men were held liable for military service . . .

Most theorists avoided the loaded question of whether increased needs for the ordinary expenses of the government could constitute an emergency. St. Thomas, it is true, suggested that permanently increased needs might qualify as an emergency and justify the imposition of permanent new taxes, and early in the fourteenth century, an Avignonese jurist, Olradus de Ponte[1] insisted that the recurrent needs of administration justified the imposition of annual taxes, which must be paid for the public utility and the needs of the kingdom. Other theorists were less helpful to the sovereign and left such phrases as "evident necessity" and the like to be interpreted broadly by kings and narrowly by their subjects.

If Philip the Fair had been able to translate directly into practice even a moderately liberal interpretation of these phrases, he would have been in an enviable position. As soon as war or another emergency occurred, he could simply have proclaimed his right to demand his subjects' service to defend the realm or graciously have allowed them to redeem their obligation by a money payment; thereupon, lines of men would have marched out against the enemy and a stream of money would have flowed into the treasury. . . . The situation was, however, a good deal more complex than this. During the thirteenth century, the study of moral theology was just as flourishing as the study of the law, and some of the same theologians and canonists who were commenting on the ruler's sovereign rights were also busily formulating elaborate theories of the justifiability and ultimate morality of men's actions. Their minds were not compartmentalized, and their moral theories greatly influenced their political ideas. Commentaries on the morality of the actions of the ruler were found in *Summas, quodlibets,*[2] and special treatises, but they were set forth most fully and most explicitly, with numerous illustrations and exhaustive examination of hypothetical cases, in the manuals written by and for confessors...

All the theorists, even the most secular minded, agreed that the imposition of unjust, extortionate taxes was *ipso facto* proof of tyranny; the ruler who overstepped the prescribed limits was committing rapine and was putting his soul in peril of eternal damnation... How to avoid this awful fate? The first sign of penance should be restitution of the unjust taxes which had been taken, and the restitution should be made to the people from whom the money had been taken. If this was impossible, the money should be put to charitable uses or spent for the common utility. Pierre Dubois[3]... wrote that it was a mortal sin for the king to ask for more aid than he needed or to request support when he did not absolutely have to have it. When the need ceased, collection of the tax must cease at once; if more was taken, the king and his officials were committing rapine, were guilty of mortal sin, and were bound to restore any excess they had taken, as a first step to penance... The crux of the matter, then, was the justice of the demand, the justifiability of the project for which the money was asked, and the responsiblity for making this decision was the king's alone...

These, then, were the needs, theories, and traditions within which Philip the Fair and his sons had to operate, and as the events of their reigns show, they were influenced fully as much by the doctrines expressed and the attitudes implicit in their confessional literature as by the ideas of more worldly minded thinkers... By 1314, the year Philip IV died, the monarchy had failed to realize its theoretical claim to discretionary judgment of the needs of the realm, and the king had acknowledged severe limitations on his rights... The king's control over the property of his subjects had been so restricted that he was basically dependent on the weakness, tolerance, good will, and understanding of his subjects to secure funds, unless the emergency was actual warfare.

Had Philip's reign ended in 1304, his accomplishments might have seemed considerably more impressive, for between 1294 and 1304, a period of continuous conflict with England and Flanders, the monarchy appeared to have developed a workable formula for securing the financial aid and military support of the realm. In these years, Philip called out armies and collected money repeatedly, and to do so he invoked the needs of the kingdom, the honor and good state of all subjects and the realm, the natural and legal obligation of all to come to the defense of the king and kingdom. Much was accomplished in the name of theoretical right and duty.

On the other hand, Philip did not simply allege and proclaim. He also wheedled, consulted, and bargained, in person and through his agents. Promises of reform were issued, privileges were confirmed, proceeds of impositions were shared with subjects who could force their dependents to pay. Even so, resistance was encountered again and again, and it was not unusual for the government to fail to press for collection and service when protests were too strong. By the end of the period it was clear that even when necessity was evident and a whole battery of conciliatory tactics was used, the monarchy could find itself at the mercy of the subjects who were in fact furnishing the service and paying the subventions.

It had also become evident that the king's subjects could be wary and quite shrewd. By 1305, groups of clergy, townsmen, and nobles had made promises of service and money which were contingent on the existence of actual conflict; service would halt and collection of subsidy cease as soon as peace was proclaimed or a truce concluded. These subjects did not deny their duty to defend the realm and aid the king in an obvious national emergency; they were not prepared, however, to accept any responsibility for or share in supporting less spectacular needs and policies of the king, nor were they willing to admit any liability to help the monarchy liquidate long-term debts incurred in the course of national emergencies.

If the theory that subjects owed support only during actual warfare became popular and gained general acceptance, the government would find it impossible to accustom its subjects to contribute to its recurrent, ordinary needs and would be unable to develop sustained habits of support. In 1305, however, the government had not acknowledged the universal applicability of any such principle, although it had admitted it in specific cases, to secure pledges of aid from various groups and individuals. By insisting repeatedly on its right to order emergency action for the good of the kingdom and by refusing to admit any general theoretical limitation of this right, the monarchy had maintained itself in a relatively strong position. It was still free to define emergency as it thought fit and employ all the propaganda and bargaining devices at its disposal to enforce its interpretation. Under favorable circumstances, Philip and his ministers might have been able to expand the royal conception of the prerogative, but events worked against them.

After 1305 came peace with Flanders, and the king therefore lacked the excuse he had so long had for experimenting with extraordinary taxation. Furthermore, in succeeding years, he profited from various nonrecurring sources of income—the confiscation of the property of the Templars and the Jews, and an aid on the marriage of his daughter. Philip and his ministers managed to make ends meet, and it may well have been to the king's ultimate disadvantage that they were able to do so. The years of peace did nothing to remind Philip's subjects of their duty to aid the king in a national emergency.

From the standpoint of the government's need to formulate and popularize a broad principle to justify extraordinary taxation, the next emergency came at an inopportune moment. It occurred in 1313, when the king was beginning to gather a feudal aid for the knighting of Louis of Navarre[4] ... Knighting and crusading festivities had provided an appropriately bellicose atmosphere for discussing the Flemish situation, which was steadily deteriorating, and Philip was able to persuade his prelates and barons that the kingdom should tolerate the disobedience of the Flemings no longer. The delinquents should be forced to fulfill the pledges they had sworn to carry out ...

This situation had many favorable aspects. It had all the signs of being exploitable to advance the monarchy's immediate and long-range financial interests. Not only were Philip's subjects bound to pay an aid for the knighting, but the threatening emergency in Flanders seemed capable of being used to justify a general demand for support. If the people of the realm could have been induced to muster or contribute when the king and his magnates judged preparatory measures necessary to avoid conflict, a notable advance would have been made toward the principle that all subjects were responsible for the general well-being and sustained protection of the kingdom, rather than merely for last-ditch support after a manifest crisis had developed. On the other hand, the situation had its dangers: a two-pronged campaign for funds and service meant double pressure on the kingdom which might well arouse resistance ...

By July 31, however, the king's ministers reached an agreement with the Flemings, and their successful diplomacy jeopardized the long-range interests of the monarchy. Philip immediately began issuing orders commanding those who had set out for Flanders to return home and informing his officials that, because peace had been preserved, they were not to take money or anything else for the campaign. The crucial step was taken two weeks later, however, for it was then that Philip commanded his agents to hand back everything they had taken, without delay. Although some money was retained, much of it seems to have been returned. The government did not count on the proceeds of the war subsidy in planning expenses for 1314, and collectors in Nîmes are known to have given back all they had gathered ...

Convenient and popular as this action may have been, there is no evidence that Philip was so hardpressed that he had to take it, and it seems clear that he was responding, however reluctantly, to the dictates of conscience rather than to practical political considerations in cancelling the tax. Consistent as this step may have been with current ethical norms, it endangered the important principle of the discretionary royal right to order armed service for the good of the realm, for it showed that the king sympathised with his subjects' reluctance to contribute to the defense of the kingdom except in cases of absolute crisis, and suggested that he shared the scruples which had prompted his Merovingian predecessors to burn their tax rolls to appease an angry God. By commanding general restitution of the money which had been gathered, and by stating explicitly that he was acting because peace had been arranged, Philip was taking, on his own initiative, a stand which could imperil the monarchy's financial well-being and severely restrict its exercise of the prerogative.

Philip seemed to be admitting that since no actual armed encounter had taken place, the monarchy was not justified in collecting a tax.

It might have been impolitic to continue the levy after the truce had been concluded, but had the government simply retained the money already taken, such action would have implied that, having issued his call to arms in good faith, the king had every right to expect his subjects to support wholeheartedly his efforts to forestall a potential threat to the kingdom, whether or not the threat actually materialized. It would also have suggested that the men of the kingdom had some obligation to help the king liquidate debts incurred while preparing defensive measures. As it was, Philip appeared to be acknowledging openly that his subjects had no such duty to him and that he had no claim to their money, property, or service unless the country was actually at war.

Cancelling the tax did not noticeably facilitate collection of the knighting aid. Although in some parts of the country the aid was paid, in other areas the king's demands were met with stubborn resistance . . .

Events of the spring of 1314 did little to raise the prestige of the monarchy. Jacques de Molay, the Grand Master of the Templars, was cruelly executed in Paris in the middle of March. He died a martyr's death, calling on God to take vengeance on those who had wrongly condemned him. Soon afterwards, scandal touched the royal family itself, for Philip's daughters-in-law were condemned for adultery and imprisoned, while their lovers were tortured to death. These events were soon the talk of the kingdom. A less propitious time for the monarchy to be forced to demand the support of the realm could hardly be conceived of, but in July the Flemings attacked the French garrison in Courtrai, and war could not be avoided.

Philip had little choice save to brazen through. It seems clear that when he and his advisors heard of the surprise attack—probably about the middle of July—they decided that immediate action was necessary and that no formal condemnation was needed, since, through their faithlessness, the Flemings had brought upon themselves the conditional sentences of excommunication and interdict which Clement V had issued in 1313.[5] Such at least is the implication of the letters which flowed from the royal chancery at the end of July and the beginning of August, summoning the men of France to appear at Arras on September 8. In these letters Philip described the evils of the Flemings and then presented himself, and by extension the subjects upon whom he was calling for support, as instruments of papal vengeance, thus suffusing his commands with an aura of righteousness they would not otherwise have had, and also avoiding the embarrassing fact that he was not claiming the formal counsel and explicit approval of the magnates of the realm for his action. In the mandates he emphasized his subjects' duty to defend the king, towns, and kingdom, and to protect the right and honor of the king and crown of France; in letters to the clergy he stressed the bond of fealty "which bound them naturally to the king." It is true that in a general letter issued on August 6 the king referred vaguely to "deep deliberation with our Council," but he laid greater stress on the fact that the defense of the kingdom "touched all his subjects" and he did not state, as he had often done in the past, that his councillors had specifically approved his decision.

Philip's failure to stress the principle of counsel and consent and his emphasis on his own emergency rights make it ironic that many historians have associated the war subsidy of 1314 with the very principle which he seems to have been evading. These writers have postulated that he called an assembly of city representatives to give their consent to the campaign against the Flemings and to the tax which would be needed to support it. It seems extremely unlikely, however, that this was the case. Instead, the king and his advisers apparently decided to take advantage of the presence in the capital of numerous townsmen who were probably there to counsel the king on the perennial problem of the coinage, to try to arouse at least a measure of enthusiasm for the coming war ... It seems clear that the assembly was little more than a set-piece planned to impress provincials and send them home full of martial ardor, for Philip had already summoned his subjects to arms ...

On August 6, Philip sent commissioners to all parts of the kingdom to call his subjects out for muster and to arrange financial compositions with them. In secret instructions he told his agents quite specifically how much he expected various categories of people to give. As in the past, a general summons to arms was being used as a device to obtain money, and this seems to have been exactly what Philip's subjects expected. When royal officials in the south tried to force the men of one town to set out for Flanders, they were flatly refused and were told that "it was not possible or customary, nor would it be profitable to the king for the men of the town to go to the army"; instead the townsmen offered paid substitutes, a gift, or a loan. In many areas of the country, opposition to the campaign and the subsidy appeared ... The situation was not improved when a temporary settlement with the Flemings was reached on September 3, and Philip may soon have rued his precipitate action of 1313. The situation in 1314 was embarrassingly similar to the circumstances of the previous year, and he was in no position to cancel the levy. The army was disbanded, but Philip still needed money to pay the men who had marched to Flanders and to cover many additional expenses. Therefore he made a desperate effort to persuade his subjects to continue to support him, despite the fact that in 1313 he had implicitly rejected the principle which could have justified his demands. On 10 September 1314, four days after Charles of Valois[6] had accepted the peace terms in Philip's name, the king wrote to officials in Amiens, describing his great need for money and commanding them to take payments from all who had not marched to Flanders. Blatantly distorting the truth, he said that he had "heard" that peace negotiations were being conducted; he did not admit that the war effort was in fact over. In other areas he did not make even this concession to public opinion. The tax continued to be collected, and musters were held in some parts of the South in mid-September. The king did all he could to second his agents' efforts, by issuing letters of nonprejudice and privilege, but general resistance developed. On October 7 the shrewd officials of Nîmes protested that the king could not intend his commissioners to take their money, since war had ceased; it was much more likely, they said, that he wanted their financial commitments cancelled. To support their position, they recalled the situation in 1313, when the subsidy had been returned after the war ended. For their pains, they were thrown into prison, and the town eventually paid 400 pounds.

Philip had obviously gambled that his subjects had forgotten or would disregard his action in 1313. Even when he found that they had not, he made no attempt to distinguish between the circumstances of the two years but simply continued to compromise and procrastinate, probably hoping that his subjects would eventually calm down and pay. Harsh measures were necessary in Auvergne, however, and the king instructed his collectors there to imprison and seize the property of men who had not tried to go to Flanders or had attempted to arouse opposition to the campaign.

Hostility to the monarchy increased, and early in November, soon after the king had suffered a minor heart attack and stroke, nobles converged from many parts of the kingdom to protest against his taxes and demand the return of all that had been taken. Probably as a result of complaints he had received, Philip issued a letter on November 16 to his agents in various parts of the South—and perhaps in other areas as well—telling them to put a temporary halt to the subsidy collection and ordering them to summon all who claimed immunity from the tax to appear before Parlement on February 16 to defend themselves. Although the letter ended on a note of hesitancy and compromise, Philip began by asserting his right to the subsidy, which, he claimed, the necessity of protecting the kingdom fully justified. Although his earlier letters of 1314 had studiously avoided discussion of principle, he now firmly announced that it was the royal right to have the tax and he implied that he might one day resume collection. On the other hand, at the end of the letter he commanded his officials to store the money they had collected until his right to the subsidy had been finally determined. This of course implied that it might be declared null and void when judgment was given in Paris, which was a perilous admission for a politician to make . . .

The North and East were in ferment. Alliances to resist the king's tax had been formed in Champagne and Burgundy early in November, and . . . the king and his councillors, in a final attempt to quiet the resentment in the kingdom, cancelled the war subsidy. Instead of simply halting collection of the tax of 1314 as an act of special grace without explaining the action, the king and his ministers again proclaimed the principle which Philip had advanced in 1313. They stated that he was stopping the tax because of his subjects' discontent and because "as he believed, his wars were over and ended." Thus, on his death-bed—for Philip died on November 29, the day after the letter was issued—the king gave the royal seal of approval to the principle limiting extraordinary taxes to wartime. When he distorted hard fact to assert that he had acted because he *believed* the war was over, although it was common knowledge that the war had ended three months before, he virtually admitted that the tax should have been cancelled in September.

Such, then, was Philip's legacy to his successor, Louis X. Statements which all but acknowledged that subjects had no obligation to defend the realm except during periods of open warfare, the prospect of cases of special privilege to be tried in Parlement, the suggestion that the court might deny the king's right to war subsidy altogether: the outlook for the prerogative was unpromising, whatever the legists and philosophers might say about utility and the needs of the kingdom . . .

Notes

1. Avignon, on the Rhone river, was in Provence, just across the border of the medieval French kingdom. It became the seat of the papacy shortly after 1305 and as such was a center for legal studies as well as finance and diplomacy [Ed.].

2. Intellectuals of the later Middle Ages generally employed the techniques of Scholasticism, which placed great emphasis on logic or dialectic as a method of scholarly inquiry. The *quodlibet* was a familiar form of scholarly disputation. The *summa*, a more ambitious type of work, attempted to arrange and summarize all the important knowledge on some subjects [Ed.].

3. Pierre Dubois was a lawyer and political writer of the reign of Philip IV [Ed.].

4. The king's oldest son, later Louis X, had been king of Navarre since 1305, when he inherited this little Spanish kingdom from his mother [Ed.]

5. Philip IV had persuaded the pope to declare that if the Flemings rebelled they would automatically incur the penalties of the Church [Ed.].

6. Charles of Valois (1270-1325) was the king's brother and the commander of the expedition against Flanders [Ed.].

Part Six: INSECURITY, CRISIS, AND TRIUMPH: THE 14TH AND 15TH CENTURIES

Chapter 17 POLITICS AND FACTIONS UNDER PHILIP VI

RAYMOND CAZELLES (b. 1917), presently the director of the Musée Condé at Chantilly, has specialized in the study of royal governmental personnel in the fourteenth century. His articles emphasize the geographical backgrounds, family connections, and rivalries of important figures on the French political scene in this period. His major work, from which this selection is taken, is a book on the "political society" at Philip VI's court. In it, Cazelles traces the rivalries of political factions and the important changes of power in Philip's government.

In giving in [to the rebellious nobles], Philip the Fair probably had mental reservations, a plan for the future. But his death and the coming to the throne of his son Louis X did not permit him to carry them out. The baronial leagues persisted, obtained from the new monarch the confirmation of his father's reform ordinance promulgated in 1301, [and] then in 1315 [were] granted a certain number of charters whose imprecise terms aimed at protection against the arbitrariness of royal officers and unjustified impositions. The vague guarantees which they obtained appear to have sufficed for the moment to the nobles, who had confidence that the king would respect them and thought to find a supplementary protection in the organization of a council where they were well represented.

From Raymond Cazelles, *La Société politique et la crise de la Royauté sous Philippe de Valois* (Paris, 1958), pp. 36-39, 46, 51-52, 71, 413, 425, 428-433. Reprinted by permission of the author. Translated by John B. Henneman.

The "Restricted Council"—as this organ was called—seems to have existed from the reign of Louis X. It took on a new significance, however, at the death of this prince and the beginning of the regency of the count of Poitiers[1] . . . There was a period of five weeks during which there was neither king nor recognized regent in the capital of the kingdom. During this time authority was exercised by a council composed of those who called themselves "the great lords of France" and who arrogated to themselves the right of dealing with current business . . .

The count of Poitiers quickly succeeded in imposing himself as regent in Paris, but he only obtained the recognition of this position from the council of the great men in return for [granting to] a Restricted Council . . . an important part of the prerogatives of kingship: since [the crown] alone could grant general pardons and, more especially, nominate to offices and present to ecclesiastical benefices. Here is an instance of a real, albeit temporary, dismemberment of monarchical power, for what authority would a regent possess who could neither name his officials, nor, on his own initiative, make any kinds of gifts to those who deserved them?

The "Restricted Council" which received these important attributes was composed of twenty-four persons. We find on it six princes of the lilies . . . two great barons . . . and two foreign princes. . . . The remainder consisted of great officers of the crown; servants of the monarchy, like Mile de Noyers, Gille Aycelin, and Raoul Rousselet; and several collaborators of the new regent, like Henri de Sully and Anseau de Joinville. The essentials of the council of the great men of France were thus retained in the Restricted Council which continued it. Certain of the people who made up this council, like Charles of Valois, Charles of La Marche, and Robert of Artois,[2] showed little sympathy for the regent; but nothing proves that they induced the whole membership of this council to share their views or their reservations. We do not know of any clashes between Philip the Tall and this council that, having wearied of the role that had been designed for it and [being] little suited to play it, would soon accept its transformation into a "monthly council," thence to be lost in the vague terminology of "great council," to which the king summoned, as did his ancestors, those who pleased him when he judged it appropriate.

The most important problem, in which the members of this "council of the great men," or "Restricted Council," could not avoid being involved, was that of the succession of Louis X. The latter died leaving a daughter of his first marriage with Margaret of Burgundy, whose misconduct rendered the [daughter's] legitimacy a little suspect. His second wife, Clementia of Hungary, was pregnant . . . An assembly composed of princes, peers, prelates, and barons . . . decided that if Clementia of Hungary had a son, Philip the Tall would keep the government of the kingdom until the majority of this son. In case of the birth of a daughter, the regent would be able to keep this government until the daughters of Louis X "came of age" . . . In the night of 13-14 November 1316, Clementia of Hungary gave birth to a boy who died after five days of reign. The treaty of July had regulated the succession of Louis X but not that of his son, and the regent, with the agreement of his uncle, Charles of

Valois, had himself recognized as king and crowned at Reims on 9 January 1317...

The crises of the reign of Philip VI [Philip of Valois, r. 1328-1350] were in gestation under Louis X and Philip V. Charles IV (r. 1322-1328), for his part, would profit from the exclusion of women to succeed his brother, but his reign, happy although brief, seems only to have added a problem (an old one, but complicated again under his reign), that of the English fiefs of Guyenne,[3] which would render still more difficult for Philip of Valois the solution of the questions raised by his accession. Already extremely ticklish under the Capetians, Anglo-French relations would become insoluble when dynastic pretensions were added to them...

Having become ill, Charles the Fair was bedridden on Christmas day of the year 1327. Since his death did not occur until 1 February 1328, the princes and magnates had time during this illness to envisage the possible situations and prepare their plans...

Edward III, the young king of England... did not contest the rule that no woman could reign in France. In effect it was not his mother Isabella, daughter of Philip the Fair and sister of the last three Capetians, who was proposed for the throne. It was he himself who claimed it, since, he said, he was more closely related to the throne than Philip of Valois, which was incontestable since [Edward] was the nephew of Charles IV while Philip of Valois was only the latter's first cousin. His arguments, presented by his partisans and lawyers, did not succeed in convincing the princes and the barons... The juridical arguments were probably less powerful to the assembly than certain sentimental reactions... Perhaps the decisive argument, although no chronicler has said so, [was] the fact that the accession of the son of Isabella to the throne of France threatened to create an inextricable situation for the future. To recognize the capacity of Philip the Fair's daughter to transmit a right she could not exercise would be to recognize it equally for all the daughters of the Capetian family, notably those who were closer to the last kings than was Isabella. None of these had a child yet, but it was very probable that they would. Thus, once crowned king of France, Edward III would be invited to step aside if one of his cousins gave the world a boy, since this boy would be a grandson of the last kings of France while Edward was only a nephew. The peril was not imaginary; Joan and Philip of Evreux would in 1332 have a son who would be the future Charles the Bad,[4] and who would not forget, later, to notice that if he was nearer to the last Capetians than Philip of Valois, he was also closer than Edward III. The wisdom of the assembly of 1328 was in having foreseen that the recognition of Edward of England could not fail to involve the kingdom in a series of crises in the name of the very principle which it would have recognized...

Philip the Tall had usurped the throne in 1317, relying on the fidelity of his partisans alone. In 1328 Philip of Valois obtained his designation as regent, and then as king, by preliminary discussions and transactions. If Philip the Tall had negotiated, after his crowning, from a situation of strength, the Valois, on the contrary, waited to have himself crowned until the peers and magnates had given him their approval. He found himself henceforth the prisoner of his promises and could not take important decisions without the consent of his barons. This became clear with the question of restoring the count of Flanders to the possession of his county.

In the first years of his reign, at least, Philip VI was not the absolute master of his decisions... Already, in 1329, he apologized to an envoy of Edward III for the fragility of his power which did not permit him to restore lands taken by his predecessors; a little later an Englishman informed his master that Philip VI did not have the authority necessary to prevent his agents and justices from intervening in the affairs of English Gascony. An innovative policy was difficult under such conditions, even for an undisputed sovereign. [One] was, however, attempted, and it succeeded for two years, from 1331 to the end of 1333. But those whom one could call the "war party" ended by frustrating it, and this defeat of the king in his council carried the germs of the future misfortunes of the reign and that of his son...

Philip of Valois never confided in one all-powerful favorite, never abandoned his power to an absolute minister. He only agreed to turn over a part of his responsibilities, when it became necessary, to one or several counsellors. Having succeeded to the throne by birth, no doubt, but also through the efforts of some and the acquiescence of others, he knew himself to be the hostage of his electors. Almost as a spectator, he was present at the intrigues and struggles of individuals and groups who wanted to take power, without compromising himself with one or with the other...

The origin of the movements which surrounded the middle of the fourteenth century must be sought before the accession of the Valois, at least as far back as the ordinance of 1303 for the reform of the kingdom, issued shortly after the defeat of Courtrai. [It] remained current fifty years later when, after it had been confirmed once by Louis X, John the Good [John II] renewed its force in the month of October 1351 and in May 1355. But the revolutions of these times did not merely spring from more or less general assemblies and from the grievances they expressed which were given satisfaction in the form of ordinances. Other problems were added to these. The position of Charles the Bad was due, certainly, to personal rancors, but he gathered around him the discontent of a whole part of political society...

There was not a struggle of one class against another, of bourgeoisie against nobility. There was a conflict between the privileged, the king's men, councillors, familiars [on the one hand], and those who not only had no access to the sharing of favors but who still paid for them; between those who intended that none of the habits of royalty be changed, since they profited from them, and those who demanded reforms and required that guarantees be given them as to the duration of these reforms, since they were weary of promises which were kept only for several months or, at best, for several years.

During the reign of Philip of Valois, kingship went through a difficult period. The crises through which it passed became more and more grave in extent as the years went by. In 1328 the accession of the Valois encountered a certain opposition, but the victory of Cassel and the homage of Amiens quickly stabilized the situation; the trial and rebellion of Robert of Artois then provoked a backlash that was appeased with greater difficulty. The events of 1340 and especially of 1343 were more dangerous, and Philip VI had to resign himself to settling with his adversaries by agreeing to truces. Finally at Crécy the king risked the loss of his kingdom.[5] Edward III, on the other hand, assumed more and more assurance in his struggle ... It was not until 1337 that he timidly took the title of king of France, to proclaim it in a striking way in 1340; after 1346, with more audacity, he might perhaps have succeeded in entering Paris or having himself crowned at Reims. French kingship seemed to weaken slowly from 1328 to 1347. This crisis of kingship was in the first place the dispute over the throne by two relations whose rivalry and possible legitimacy left to the subjects the task and duty of choosing between one or the other, giving clever and ambitious persons the opportunity of putting their fealty at auction. But it was also a succession of protests against those clever and ambitous [persons] who succeeded in installing themselves in power and diverting to their own profit the favors of the monarchy. The crisis of royalty did not, however, overtake the monarchy itself or its power. One would rather reproach the king with not using it more fully, of acting only through the intermediary of his counsellors. The king remained the one recourse, and no rule could limit his authority. Kingship was in full crisis, but the fullness of royal power remained intact. The kingdom aspired to be governed by a firm hand ...

It was not so much at the king as at his council that the public aimed their protests. In this regard, the reign of Philip VI has left us an original attempt at the reorganization of this council. There already existed, before the Valois, sovereigns of the Chamber of Accounts; Enguerrand de Marigny seems to have occupied this function; Mile deNoyers under Louis X and Henri de Sully under Philip V certainly possessed the title. This was an extremely important, essential post, which made its occupant the chief of the whole financial administration. He directed not only the masters of the accounts but also the treasurers and receivers, and he corresponded directly with the bailiffs and seneschals. After the death of Philip the Tall, Charles IV, who relied especially on his treasurer, seems not to have retained the function of sovereign of the Chamber of Accounts for several years. It is only in 1326 that we find a new mention of sovereigns of the accounts, and the office is divided, since it had two holders, between Mile de Noyers, who regained his old post, and the constable Gaucher de Châtillon ... The old counsellors of Philip of Valois did not intend to be deprived of the advantages they anticipated from the fact of having served the king before his accession. The sovereignty of the Chamber of Accounts was then such a small thing that after 1332 Mile de Noyers resided far from court for much of the time. But a total change is evident around 1335-1336, and Noyers soon joined the presidency of the Chamber of Accounts with the office of Butler of

France... Henceforth one can truly speak of a college of sovereigns of the Chamber of Accounts and... this college became the Great, or Secret, Council, acquiring new members without losing old ones except by death, until there were ten in 1345. The novelty is not that there was a council; it is that this council was organized around the Chamber of Accounts and that the members of it were of a limited number, that they received special salaries for their service, that they generally resided in Paris for their work, and that they were retained by the king in the position of permanent councillors.

Except for an ephemeral attempt under Philip the Tall, the royal council had not been organized by the last Capetians. The king called it together when he wanted to and called to it those whom he wished. The press of business naturally weighed on the sovereigns of the Chamber of Accounts, the Keeper of the Seal, the royal officers on fixed sojourn in the capital. Nearly all political matters had financial aspects, and naturally the bulk of them were submitted to the sovereigns of the Chamber of Accounts and the treasury who, in the king's absence, made numerous decisions by themselves. It is probably against this omnipotence of one or two men that there was constituted this college of sovereigns who inherited directly the functions of [such men as] Marigny, Sully, and Noyers. What was organized was a real government, in which participated the only councillors retained by the king, to whom were joined at times the princes or the great officers of the crown.

On still closer examination of the facts, we perceive that inside this college a small nucleus kept the essential tasks to itself... The other members either were merely honorary councillors or had some other duties which kept them from coming regularly to the council. Thus, of itself, the council avoided being transformed into a crowd and remained faithful to its original character of restrictiveness in spite of royal promotions. It is possible that in the end the situation was not very different from what it had been under the last Capetians.

The very particular association of the council and the Chamber of Accounts ceased on 14 December 1346. The Chamber was asked to confine itself to its accounting role, and the members of the secret council lost their positions as sovereigns. The secret council, somewhat modified, continued its career, however... It seems that the Estates of 1356, when they protested against the fact that those who governed were "only two or three persons," were resisting a natural law of this time which willed that a restricted commission emerge from among the king's councillors in order to administer the kingdom.

The organization of this council of sovereigns cast a great luster on the Chamber of Accounts, which become the essential organ of the French monarchy. This elevation eclipsed another organ, the *Parlement*. The Chamber of Accounts represented the tradition of Philip the Fair, under whose reign it rose into full view, and of his son Philip the Tall, who gave it its status. The *Parlement* was traditional royalty in the exercise of justice; it represented the memory of Saint Louis, whose reign appeared, with the passage of time, as a happy and equitable period whose memory was nostalgically preserved. These great bodies were rivals, and favor or interest fell upon first one and then the other. For several years the *Parlement* benefited from the accession of Philip of Valois who, after 1328, had some of his most faithful friends preside over it ... The first conflicts occurred under the chancellorship of Guillaume de Sainte-Maure, (who was), however, favorable to the people of the *Parlement* ... When the council of the sovereigns of the Chamber of Accounts was organized, the *Parlement* progressively lost its prestige and authority. We know of the effacement of this institution in 1339 and 1340, then its progressive reestablishment thereafter. Insofar as the Chamber of Accounts saw its influence restricted, the *Parlement*, which succeeded in being regulated by highly favorable ordinances, gained in prestige, to the point of imposing its leaders on the college of sovereigns of the accounts and the requests of the household. Its personnel became permanent, virtually irremovable, since it recruited itself by co-optation. It became the essential institution of kingship, and this was one of the most durable conquests of the period which interests us, for the monarchy of the Valois would be a "monarchy of the *Parlement*."

Notes

1. Philip the Tall, count of Poitiers, was the future Philip V [Ed.].

2. These were the three leading princes. Charles of La Marche was Philip's brother, the future Charles IV. Robert of Artois was their third cousin [Ed.].

3. Guyenne was the reduced duchy of Aquitaine still held by the English king in southwestern France [Ed.].

4. For Charles the Bad, and all other persons involved in the succession question, see the genealogical table at the front of the book.

5. At the battle of Crécy (August 1346), Philip was disastrously defeated by the English. In 1343 he had faced scattered rebellion and opposition to his coinage policy but had won over the opposition with timely concessions [Ed.].

Chapter 18 THE PANIC AND DEFEAT OF JOHN II

EDOUARD PERROY (b. 1901), professor at the Sorbonne, is one of the most distinguished French medievalists of this century. He taught at British universities for more than a decade, and he has made a specialty of Anglo-French relations in the later middle ages. He is equally prominent as an economic and social historian of late medieval France, but Americans know him best for his history of the Hundred Years' War, from which this selection is taken. The book was written while he was working in the French Underground during World War II, and it is appropriate to reprint here his account of another dark episode of his country's history.

The death of Philip VI, in August 1350, brought to the throne his son John, whom posterity has nicknamed the Good. . . . The disasters into which he plunged, head down, were to modify his contemporaries' opinion of him. He was reproached with surrounding himself with councillors of low birth, who were incompetent, greedy, mindful only of their own fortunes, such as Robert of Lorris, Nicholas Braque, Simon of Bucy. Yet some of them had already been his father's councillors, and others were to surround his son. If his reign had been fortunate, he would have been congratulated on his choice. Froissart[1] . . . explains John's failure by his defects of character. These were doubtless real, but they do not tell the whole story. John was quick to take offence, and subject to terrible rages which were provoked

From *The Hundred Years War* by Edouard Perroy (translated by W. B. Wells, 1951), pp. 125-133. Reprinted by permission of the Indiana University Press. (Bloomington, Ind.: Indiana University Press, 1951).

by the vaguest suspicions. He struck without rhyme or reason at those whom he distrusted, and was incapable of letting these irrational hatreds subside. His harsh justice was to the taste of the men of his time, but it was not balanced by pardons generously granted. If this caused indignation, it was because the king was not lucky in his enterprises. People went so far as to mutter the strangest accusations against him. The favor he showed some upstarts, notably the Constable Charles of Spain, was put down to moral obliquity. Posterity has not yet done justice to all these calumnies.

The misfortune was that, at a tragic moment in its history, the crown of France was worn, not by an incapable man—the epithet would be too strong—but by a mediocrity. John was conscious, to be sure, of the dangers he ran, but he lacked sufficient strength of mind to face them. He lived in a state of permanent panic, in an atmosphere of treachery, which we must bear in mind if we are to understand his brutal acts of revenge. Yet, despite the blows of fate, despite the drain of the "pestilence," the kingdom remained rich and powerful ... Preliminary defeats did not seem to have touched the country in its vitals. Accordingly John's court remained the meeting place of the knights of Europe in quest of tourneys and feasts. It carried on the life of festivity which it had spent under Philip VI ...

But this brilliant façade hid deep cracks. The social and economic crisis produced by the plague of 1348 had lasting repercussions which no one knew just how to check. It was thought advisable to enact legislation about wages, restore them to the pre-plague level, prevent the workers from leaving their masters, compel slackers to take work at low rates, on pain of being branded with a red-hot iron. All this was of no avail. The ordinance of 1351, unlike the English statutes on the same subject, does not appear to have been vigorously enforced. In the countryside, the lords witnessed the flight of their depleted labour from their lands and accused the government of ruining them. No one knew how to face renewal of the war, which John seemed fearfully to anticipate with terror. It was essential in the first place to discipline the army. An ordinance, also issued in 1351, established a new scale of pay for knights banneret, knights bachelor, and squires, fixed at twenty-five the minimum number of men-at-arms marching in "route" under the banner of any captain,[2] and ordered bimonthly reviews, held without previous notice by the marshals' clerks, in order to avoid frauds in connexion with the strength and armament of the companies.

All this led to next to nothing, because the government was unable to provide regular pay, and as a result the captains disbanded their men in excess of the legal minimum and all of them lived on the country. The royal coffers remained empty, and the people, more than decimated by war and epidemics, refused to pay taxes. At every meeting of the Estates, in Languedoc and Paris alike, there was nothing but jeremiads over the exactions of the king's officials and refusals of grants by the members, who pleaded the impoverishment of their provinces or claimed that they had no mandate to pledge their constituents. The economic crisis and the financial crisis drove the government to fresh monetary "mutations," which, in less than six years, devalued the royal currency, already very weak, by 70 percent.

So it was essential, at all costs, to prevent the war from flaring up again in such unfavourable conditions. It was necessary to deal pitilessly with all those who, directly or indirectly, seemed to favour the enemy's cause. Into this policy of panic John flung himself recklessly and clumsily, with no resources other than his own mediocre brain, influenced by an entourage which sponged on him. The years 1350-1356 were among the most incoherent in a century sufficiently fertile in delusions.

Edward III was not unaware of the weaknesses and the panic fear of the new King of France. He took pleasure in prolonging the threat, continually postponed, of a fresh landing . . .

Then an ally more dangerous for the Valois presented himself to Edward. This was Charles of Navarre, son of Joan of France and Philip of Évreux, "prince of the lilies on all sides," and soon to become the mortal enemy of the dynasty which reigned in Paris. When he came on the scene, he was still only a youth, but an attractive one, a glib talker, intelligent and madly ambitious. As grandson, through his mother, of the last direct Capetians, his rights to the throne of France took precedence of those of the Plantagenets. One day he was to regret that he had not been born earlier. In 1328, he would doubtless have been preferred to the lacklustre Valois . . .

But what could he do against the powerful French monarchy? What was the little kingdom of Navarre and a few Norman fiefs in comparison with France? He could derive strength only from intrigue. To get in touch with the King of England, promise to help the Plantagenet's cause, talk if need be about a partition of France with the English pretender, and then, when surprise and fear had taken effect, become reconciled with the Valois and wrest fresh territorial concessions from him—such was the policy of this perpetual conspirator. It was a policy lacking in grandeur or frankness, the policy of a man who doubted his own strength and played someone else's game without winning his own.

But what a wonderful instrument for Edward III! It so happened that John the Good, not content with entrusting Charles of Spain . . . with the Constable's sword which had fallen from the hand of Raoul of Brienne, executed for "treason," also gave him the county of Angoulême, which Charles of Navarre regarded as his own. Early in 1354, Charles—his Spanish subjects were later to call him *el Malo*, the Bad—and his younger brothers lured the favourite into an ambush. As he was passing through Laigle, in their Norman lands, they had him savagely murdered. The king, in his grief and fury, swore revenge on the Navarrese brothers. But Charles secured the interest in his cause of his aunt and his sister, the widows of Charles IV and Philip VI, and got the Pope and others to intervene. Making plenty of noise about it, he got into touch with the English, and sought the armed aid of Henry, Duke of Lancaster, Edward III's cousin and his lieutenant for French affairs.

"Know that it was I," he confessed insolently, "who, with the help of God, had Charles of Spain killed." Faced with the formidable collusion of rebel and enemy, the King of France swallowed his pride, and allowed the Cardinal of Boulogne, that self-seeking courtier, to arrange a reconciliation. Charles was restored to favour. As the price of his submission, he was given a good part of Cotentin. The Treaty of Mantes (March 1354) humiliated the King of France without appeasing his insatiable son-in-law . . .

A last drama heralded final disaster. Charles of Navarre, still dissatisfied with his lot, had resumed his intrigues. In the autumn of 1355, when he was in his domain in Cotentin, he planned to cross over to England. Once more the king managed to appease him by the Treaty of Valognes. Then he established himself in Rouen and struck up a dangerous friendship with the Dauphin Charles, who had recently been created Duke of Normandy. Rumor had it that the two young men were plotting to overthrow the king. John's stored-up hatred and suspicion could stand things no longer. Suddenly, on April 5th 1356, galloping up still breathless from a long and secret ride, the King of France burst into the room in Rouen where his son, his son-in-law, and their suite were feasting. Charles the Bad's friends were seized and executed on the spot, and he himself was thrown into a dungeon. The whole past record of its victims invited this lightning stroke, yet it created a scandal, because it came too late, after too many surrenders and feigned reconciliations and because Charles enjoyed secret and mysterious sympathizers among a nobility who were frivolous, carping, fond of intrigue, and, as usual, devoid of any political sense.

After this, events moved fast. It was learned that an English raiding force, several thousand horsemen strong and led by Henry of Lancaster, had left Brittany and was advancing upon Normandy, rightly counting on the rising of all Charles's partisans. The Black Prince's Anglo-Gascon army, five or six thousand men in all, had regrouped and invaded Poitou, burning and pillaging on its way, seeking to reach and cross the Loire, with the obvious intention of linking up with the Duke of Lancaster in his operations in Normandy. Neither of the English armies, in view of their small strength, could await a pitched battle, still less seek one. Lancaster, by clever maneuvring, managed to dodge his adversary. But when the Black Prince, who was then in Berry, learned that King John's army was making ready to pursue him, he fell back slowly towards Guienne, heavily encumbered with his booty.

About the middle of September, near Maupertuis, to the west of Poitiers on the River Miosson, he was overtaken by the French army, whose strength of perhaps 9,000 was sufficient to crush him. But two cardinals, sent by Pope Innocent VI, obtained a truce for twenty-four hours, in order to attempt, at the last minute, fruitless negotiations for peace. This providential respite was employed by the English and the Gascons to organize themselves in stronger positions. When battle was finally joined, their numerical inferiority forced them, as at Crécy, to resort to stratagems unworthy of knights: concealment along hedges, ambushes in woodland, fire of the Welsh archers which decimated the enemy's horses, feints to lure on their various "battles" one by one. Before the combat, the Black Prince would have asked nothing better than to withdraw into his own domain, even promising not to take up arms again for seven years, so much did he fear disaster in face of his enemy. But, when the three days' struggle was over, on September 19th, those of the French who had not fallen or fled found themselves prisoners of a smaller Anglo-Gascon army. Its Gascon leaders, such as the lord (*captal*) of Buch, and Chandos, much more than the Prince of Wales, had been the architects of victory. Among the prisoners thrust along the road to Bordeaux was the King of France, who had persistently refused to flee . . .

The king a captive: the whole tragedy for France was summed up in those words. Such a situation had not been witnessed for more than a century . . . .

The remotest corners of all the provinces were moved to pity for the chivalrous sovereign's misfortune: proof of a loyalty to the monarchy which no mistake, no defeat could shake. But the suffering people wanted scapegoats. They turned on the nobility, heedless and reckless, who had spoiled for a fight and let themselves be crushed on the battlefields. They blamed the incompetence of the royal officials and the king's councillors, whose useless exactions from an overtaxed nation had not prevented disaster. Their hatred, though latent everywhere, did not break out everywhere. Through the interplay of circumstances, revolt found voice only in two strictly defined centres: the burgesses of Paris and the towns of Île-de-France, on the one hand; the peasantry of Beauvaisis, on the other. But the audacity of a small number often gets the better of the apathy of the masses. For nearly two years, this unrelenting opposition was to put in peril the whole royal administration, the fruit of centuries of patient effort, and perhaps even the future of the dynasty.

There was indeed a constitutional crisis. It seemed all the more dangerous because the ship was without a pilot. On the battlefield of Poitiers the king's eldest son had taken to flight. Upon this youth of eighteen, after the disaster, the lieutenancy of the kingdom now devolved. His physical weakness was patent to all eyes. A sickly youth of unpleasing appearance, married too young to his cousin Joan of Bourbon, lacking in real political experience and worthless as a soldier, Charles had hitherto been nothing but the plaything of a dubious entourage. He bore the title of Dauphin, but it was the king's officials who governed Dauphiné in his name. He had been made Duke of Normandy, but he had spent only a few months in his appanage, leading a life of careless pleasure. He had let himself be beguiled by his brother-in-law of Navarre, and perhaps had plotted with him against his father. Nothing about him foreshadowed the man of long matured plans, clever at getting out of tight corners and gambling with fate. The youth who, stiffened by misfortune, was to become Charles V seemed as yet only a pitiful puppet. He surrounded himself with King John's most decried councillors, and learned from them to become underhand. He defied unpopularity and seemed to mock the misery of the people.

Notes

1. Froissart was the famous fourteenth century chronicler of the first half of the Hundred Years' War. He was sympathetic to the English and mainly emphasized feats of chivalry [Ed.].

2. The characteristic military organization of the fourteenth century was the "company," or "route," consisting of professional fighting men who were recruited and paid by their captain, a member of the nobility. Nobles were classified as squires, knights, or knights banneret according to their wealth, experience, and military equipment, although these ranks tended to become hereditary [Ed.].

Chapter 19 THE VALOIS KINGS AND THEIR FINAL TRIUMPH

PETER S. LEWIS (b. 1931), of All Souls College, Oxford, is an expert on the political history of France in the fifteenth century, particularly the relations between the king and the aristocracy. Among his other writings, he has contributed an important article to the growing literature on the failure of the Estates General in France to develop permanent constitutional importance. The portions of his recent book on later medieval France reprinted here contain his characterization of the Valois kings and Lewis's final conclusions.

Of the king's two bodies, the public body and the private, the second was certainly human enough. The first three Valois monarchs were, on the whole, fairly normal. Philip VI as the first tenant of a disputed throne did very far from badly. "It's a reasonable thing to do, to change one's mind," he said at the end of his reign; and this ability to trim may to some extent explain his apparent inactivities as it might explain those of his descendant Charles VII. But he behaved like a king: he was active in leading his army; he was known for his vigour and his boldness. He was thought by some to be precipitate in his behaviour: the author of the *Chronique des quatres premiers Valois* thought he was "a fearfully hasty man": but most obloquy seems to have fallen on Joan of Burgundy, his wife . . ."Wicked indeed and

From P. S. Lewis, *Later Medieval France: The Polity* (London, 1969), pp. 110-118, 375-379. Reprinted by permission of St. Martin's Press, Inc., the Macmillan Company of Canada, and the Macmillan Company of London and Basingstoke.

dangerous was this queen of France, the mother of King John," wrote Froissart, "and she died a sudden death." Her son is supposed to have taken after her: he, too, had rather a bad press, though admittedly the worst of it (he "was the worst and cruelest king who ever lived, and he was moreover the son of the queen of Burgundy, who never liked Normans") appears in the fifteenth-century chronicle of the Norman Pierre Cochon: not a very trustworthy source. In the *Complainte sur la bataille de Poitiers* he appears as the paragon of military regality:

If everyone else had been as valiant as he
Beaten and made villeins the English would be

but the balance of the clerical author of the *Complainte* is also suspect. The actual behaviour of the king could only too easily be assimilated by the public image.

Charles V, his successor, has perhaps suffered from the adulation of Christine de Pisan.[1] Certainly for her "this very true Christian", "very devout and very catholic" king was almost without reproach. Illness had made him unwarlike ... but otherwise he was a model prince. Perhaps he was wiser even than Christine knew. But she could point out ... that his apparent love of ceremonious progresses "was not simply indulgence, but in order to keep, maintain and give example to his successors in time to come that in solemn order should be held and conducted the most worthy status of the high crown of France, to which all sovereign magnificence is due, pertains and must be paid" certainly ... Charles's entourage was prepared to gild it. Never angry, always moderate, imbued with political tact and loved by all, he, too, was a paragon, but of the peaceful arts. The recovery of France during his reign was an undoubted tribute to his virtues; but one should not be carried away cloud-borne into Christine's apotheosis.

The brother of Charles's wife, Louis II of Bourbon, died a melancholic, and Joan of Bourbon herself lost "her wits and her memory" for a while at the age of thirty-five in 1373. In her child Charles VI [r. 1380-1422] the weakness of the line of St. Louis came out to the full. Charles was every inch a king. Above average height, robust, broad chested, fresh faced and fair haired, he loved tournaments and was alleged to excel in military exercises. He was friendly, good tempered and generous. But the old Adam and rather more did come out in this juvenile prodigy. Carnal appetites (though never causing scandal or dishonor to a family and never violently satisfied) reminded the Religieux de St. Denis of the former; and his refusal to wear the now old-fashioned robes thought suitable for a king, his delight in disguising himself as a Bohemian or a German and his insistence in taking part in tournaments after having received unction upset the Religieux and probably others. He seems, in fact, to have been a rather retarded youth. In 1392 he went off his head. In April he had had, probably, typhoid fever at Amiens. His convalescence from this had probably been insufficient, and during it he appeared very excitable: an expedition undertaken against Pierre de Craon in Brittany was probably a product of this excitability. At the beginning of August, on his way westward, he began to behave very peculiarly. On 5 August, possibly affected by alcohol, possibly affected by sunstroke, he went raving mad in the forest of Le Mans, after a slight shock, and killed four men before his sword broke and he could be tied up. A week later he had recovered; but he was not himself until November or December. In June 1393 he was mad again, this time until January 1394; and thereafter the attacks repeated one another with monotonous regularity: his madness became the king's "usual malady."

Mania, mental confusion, depression have all been disentangled in Charles's syndrome. Even in the lucid periods the king was mentally unstable. At some times in them his grip failed: his attention, his memory and his will would wander. At other times he kept his wits about him and could be active in affairs. It was, therefore, possible for him to act independently as king; but he was a prey to those around him, great and small ... Isabeau of Bavaria, Charles's wife,

> was pretty and gracious enough
> Without a quarter or a moiety
> Of [her husband] 's very great beauty,
> For she was short and brown-colored.

Other writers could be more unkind. Reason, in the *Songe veritable*, said

> You, lady Isabeau, the queen that
> Is enveloped in horrid fat

and her ill looks, as well as the virtues and vices of the Wittelsbachs and the Viscontis,[2] were passed on to son and grandson. It will never be known for certain if the tares of the Valois were passed on to Charles VII (r. 1422-1461) by Charles VI. Louis XI once told the Neapolitan ambassador that Isabeau "was a great whore" and that Charles VII was supposed to be descended from her and Charles VI ("who was a fool") "but that he did not know whose child he was"; and allegedly Charles VII had enough doubts about his paternity until they were supposedly assuaged by Joan of Arc. But there is little real reason to suppose that Charles VII could not have been the son of his putative father, and indeed, in those much-quoted words of the saint, "true heir of France and king's son." But the mixture of Valois, Wittelsbach and Visconti, though it produced eccentrics, also produced kings of high ability.

He was thin, wrote Chastellain of Charles VII, with feeble legs and a most peculiar walk; "his face was pallid, but good looking enough, his speech good and very pleasing and subtle, not very high pitched. His demeanour was attractive and gracious." Mutability, distrust and envy were his principal failings, but his virtues, "obviously by the labour of God," made him "glorious above many of his predecessors." He undoubtedly had a number of not very important neuroses, the best documented of which is anthropophobia; but his physical health seems to have been good until the late 1450s. Remarkable diagnoses of mental instability have been produced in order to explain his alleged inactivity in the 1420s and early 1430s. But there seems little real reason to go much beyond Chastellain's analysis of Charles' character. To the Burgundian chronicler the king, far from robust, far from bellicose, was never a man to do things for himself. He relied on others; but he was capable in the end of leading them and not being led by them. The very vice of changeableness led to a fairly rapid turnover of "favourites"; the aspirant could be played off against the sitting tenant. In the end the government was made up of "bits and pieces of different people all assembled up and sewn together," who worked effectively for the public good as well as for their own and eventually threw the English out of France . . .

We know more about the personality of Charles's successor, Louis XI, [r. 1461-1483], than about any of his predecessors'. If he did nothing else, Louis had an infinite capacity for arousing hatred; it was with fear and imprecation that men remembered him. More than any of his predecessors he seems to have had a curious need and a capacity for self-expression in his words and in his actions. Italy and the ways of Italians fascinated him; deceit delighted him. A Burgundian writer christened him the universal spider. He could be both sentimental and ruthless, entranced with his own wickedness and indignant that he might be thought wicked, confident towards God and man and stricken with fear or remorse towards sentimental and ruthless, entranced with his confident towards God and man and stricken with fear or remorse toward them. He did not appear, or dress, or speak like a king; yet "he was the most terrible king who ever was" and even the trees trembled before him. It was little wonder that an Italian ambassador in 1462 said that he came out in a sweat from head to foot when he was summoned by Louis XI. Yet he could be extremely friendly; "he knew how to be pleasant when he wanted to," even at his most crotchety; he was pathologically fond of animals, especially dogs and singing-birds; his love of hunting came second only to his love of the business of kingship and international politics and sometimes even got in the way of it. Even his deepest calumniator did not deny that he was highly literate; even a rather critical Italian thought in 1479 that he cited the best authors. He shocked everyone by an extreme and even endearing informality. The Italian ambassadors, not used to such things, seemed constantly chasing miles after him to some "extremely miserable little peasant's shack" in the woods. He liked eating in taverns and with his rather peculiar friends in town. He had a cruel sense of humour; he could be unwittingly or wittingly cruel; he lacked justice of mind and he lacked loyalty, he liked adversity and he disliked concord. He "intended to be sovereign"; he "did not wish to share his kingdom." He would and could never be beaten; he would never accept for long the will of others imposed upon him. Only rarely did he think himself wrong; and then not for long. "Perhaps," he said to his doctors on the point of death, "I am not as ill as you think." But he was, and he died...

If there had been a "crisis" in French society in the later middle ages, what had been its nature? Admittedly there had been economic misfortune. Admittedly there had been social tension. But a "crisis," it may be argued, was political, and its roots were to be found in the disputed successions to the last Capetian kings of France. It was the Plantagenet claim that gave the secular conflict of the period its peculiar configuration. Behind all the manoeuvres, all the tergiversations and the treacheries of the conflict, military and diplomatic, lay the appeal or the recourse of an alternative dynasty; an appeal exercised in a state whose elements were not yet wholly fused...

The crisis... was thus fundamental. From it derived a number of other effective subjections of the crown in later medieval France. But the king of France, despite the fact that the natural resources of his country were so much greater than those of the king of England, was basically in a politically weaker position, before ever the Valois came to the throne, than the king of England. The last Capetians, unlike the Plantagenets, could not extract taxes from a single general assembly with full powers. They could not tax their nobles. And the overmightiness of the magnates of France of the older lines was apparent before the weakness of the Valois title made it even more necessary for the kings of France to placate them and their newer colleagues.

It might in fact be seen as aggression for a king to attempt to assert a greater unity; aggression even in the name of an idea, of a concept only in the later middle ages being created. It was the creation of the king's lawyers and the king's propagandists; it was they who created the myth which the king's armies realized. By a combination of good management and good fortune Aquitaine was defeated; Burgundy and Anjou died out in the direct male line, as had Berry; the line of Orléans was apparently sterilized by Louis XI's marriage of Louis II of Orléans to his deformed daughter Joan of France. Louis exulted over his enemies. "His joy was very great," wrote Commynes,[3] "to see himself on top of all those whom he hated and his adversaries. On some he was avenged, like the constable of France, the duke of Nemours and several others; the duke of Guyenne, his brother, was dead, and he had his succession; all the house of Anjou was dead, René king of Sicily, John and Nicholas dukes of Calabria, and then their cousin the count of Maine, who was later count of Provence, the count of Armagnac, who had been killed at Lectoure, and of all of them the king had collected the inheritance and the property." He had also collected part of those of the duke of Burgundy and might have collected the rest if he could have married the heiress of Charles *le teméraire* to the dauphin[4] or to some rather older seigneur who would be in his pocket. But Flanders remained beyond Louis's grasp; and the houses of Brittany, Bourbon, Orléans and Foix remained. And, though the senior branches of the first and last of these ran out into a female line in 1488 and 1483, the problem of the very great was to remain for later kings to deal with—if their families may have been different.

But the rebellion of the duke of Aquitaine and the war for the throne of France was, in 1453, effectively over. The Valois had won. Yet the crisis of the war had produced a number of problems. The hatreds it had engendered took a generation to die down. The bribes made, out of weakness, to the great for their loyalty ... and pensions long outlived the fifteenth century. The control of the civil service, the control of the army, remained a problem; and so did the promises of rebels, remained dangerous in Louis XI's eyes; and even their oligarchies might need to be watched closely. The effects of the crisis of confidence, of the crisis of control, remained to the end of his reign.

Is it then realistic to think of the crown in France by the end of the middle ages as "absolute"? First of all we must be careful in our use of the term. Although Claude de Seyssel[5] might equate absolutism with despotism, by the 1530s the term was beginning to be used to describe a true monarchy precisely of his own definition: a rule bridled by God's laws, by natural law, by fundamental laws. It was only, it has been maintained, in the arguments of seventeenth-century aristocrats and their supporters that the word became once more pejorative. But one is warned against taking the formal position for the real one. Clearly there were many things a king was powerless to do in the face of his subjects of all estates, in practice as well as in principle. His courts might effectively protect his subjects' rights against his immediate whim; and his courts and his central departments might effectively protect his own "rights," as an abstract entity, against his personal volition. The true bridles of the king of France lay in his entourage, in his agents, and in the power of those who effectively resisted them. Some, like the resistance of the Parlements or of the departments to royal actions, were formal. Some, like the backstairs intrigues and pressures of princes, great clerics and great towns, were informal. In the interplay of the forces of this political society true power was to be found and the true position of the king to be ascertained. And it is upon this complex that the effect of the crisis of confidence should be assessed.

The tyranny which men like Jean Juvenal des Ursins[6] saw in France in the fifteenth century was the tyranny of royal ineffectiveness within that complex. That ineffectiveness, admittedly, preceded the Valois crisis; but the crisis, let alone the incapacity of Charles VI, clearly enhanced it. The king of Bourges[7] could do little but be ineffective, given his political situation. The libel "tyranny" came easily into the polemic of the critical then and later. The Englishman Sir John Fortescue, for instance ... was chilled to the marrow by the governance of France ...

It was the opportunity for tyranny offered by the civil law as he conceived it that Fortescue abhorred. Many heads were better than one; and for Fortescue the salvation of England lay in parliamentary control of taxation and the statute law. Admittedly "representation stabilizes power structure by providing a mean between extremes of concentration and dispersion of power..." But what part in reality did the English Parliament play in the fifteenth century in creating that mean? How far, indeed, was Fortescue in defence of the English system *parti pris* or at the most prophetic? The activities of Parliament were hardly the whole of politics. Nor was the existence of Pariament incontrovertible. Fortescue himself seems to have been very much afraid of a "reception" of civil law; and, in the next century and later, England was not without its theorists of "absolitism" = *la françgise*' And Fortescue would still be forced to admit that the whole question turned essentially upon what the king ruling simply regally did with his powers. The absence of effective representative institutions cannot be seen in Fortescue's terms as creating an absolutism in the nonpejorative sense. Neither can it be seen as creating a despotism; for this was created by the misuse of the unfettered will, both for Fortescue and for Seyssel. For both of them tyranny was created by the negligence of such governance; Parliament was simply Fortescue's bridle for the monarch. It was the accident of the development of the English polity that it existed; and it continued to exist only because the structure of that polity allowed it to.

It is thus to a certain extent with the advantage of hindsight that one sees the French Estates and their failure as important. But the liberty of those who were politically important under the Valois kings need not have suffered unless they became the king's enemies; the oligarchs of the towns, the greater clergy, the greater nobility had their own place in the scheme of tensions and resistances that was the power complex in later medieval France. It was the more minute changes in that scheme which made political movement in the fourteenth and fifteenth centuries, not the protection of a poor taxpayer—however much his interests may have been paraded by the men of letters and their near kin, the compilers of the *cahier de doléances* of 1484.

For that society, including perhaps even its lowest members, did not, perhaps, any more than Sir John Fortescue, believe in progress. From top to bottom its members might be rebels; but they were hardly revolutionary. Even Gerson could be ashamed of his peasant origins. Nor was there much social change willy-nilly. There was a constant movement between the classes, but this does not constitute social change. There is perhaps some evidence that peasant fortunes improved with the shortage of labour from the first plague onwards; but there is also evidence that this improvement may have been short-lived. There is also evidence of the capacity of the old families to survive the misfortunes of the fourteenth and fifteenth centuries. The social realities of the period matched its general political theory. Out of the long decades of tribulation had emerged a sentimental attachment to a strong ruler, whose

> safety is our safety
> And his ruin is our loss.

Nobles, churchmen, oligarchs effectively accepted the myths of monarchy. In this sense at least there was an absolute monarchy in France, an absolute monarchy by "right divine." This was the essential "recovery of France" at the end of the middle ages: the arrogation of the idea of Valois monarchy over its opponent theories to some extent in practice. The process was far from wholly deliberate, far from wholly without the intervention if not of God at least of Fortune. It was the result in part of a series of accidents, and it was in part to dominate the history of the French people to the present day.

Notes

1. Christine de Pisan (1364-ca. 1430) was the daughter of Charles V's Italian astrologer. Her writings included a laudatory account of this monarch [Ed.]

2. The Wittelsbachs were counts of Hainault and Holland in the Low Countries, as well as dukes of Bavaria. They had marriage connections with the Visconti family which ruled the Italian duchy of Milan. Queen Isabeau was thus descended from both families [Ed.]

3. Philippe de Commynes, a courtier of the duke of Burgundy, deserted his master in 1472 to become an adviser to Louis XI. He fell from favor on the king's death but later returned to court. His famous memoirs are a highly respected source for the last third of the fifteenth century [Ed.].

4. Charles *le téméraire* (the Rash; sometimes called the Bold), duke of Burgundy, 1467-1477, ruled the entire Netherlands as well as Burgundy and came close to creating an independent state between France and Germany. He was succeeded by his daughter Mary (1459-1482), who refused to consider marrying Louis XI's seven-year-old son and instead married archduke of Austria [Ed.].

5. A French official and political writer of the early sixteenth century [Ed.].

6. A French official and political writer of the early fifteenth century [Ed.].

7. Bourges was the capital of Charles VII during the years that the English occupied Paris (1420-1436) [Ed.].

Suggestions for Further Reading

Any bibliography must necessarily be selective in character. Some of the more important books about medieval France are discussed below, but only a few of the many important articles that have been written in this field are mentioned. Very few up-to-date works on medieval France are easily available in English. Despite the vast literature on the subject, there is no single-volume history of medieval France, even in French. For good general coverage, the student must still be directed to *Histoire de France*, edited by E. Lavisse, 9 vols. (Paris, 1900-1911); volumes 2-4 of this series were written by Achille Luchaire, Charles-Victor Langlois, Alfred Coville, and Charles Petit-Dutaillis, four of the giants of French medieval historiography. Also useful is the more recent series *Histoire Générale*, edited by G. Glotz, notably volumes IV-2, VI-1, VI-2, and VII-1 (Paris, 1937-1941).

In the realm of economic history, a somewhat dated but still serviceable work is H. Sée, *Histoire économique de la France*, vol. I (Paris, 1939). Monographs devoted to the medieval French towns are C. Petit-Dutaillis, *Les communes françaises* (Paris,

1947), and the older work by A. Luchaire, *Les communes françaises à l'époque des capétiens directs* (Paris, 1890). Fortunately, the two most important works on medieval agrarian history are now available in English: M. Bloch, *French Rural History: Its Original Characteristics* (Berkeley, 1966); and G. Duby, *Rural Economy and Country Life in the Medieval West* (London, 1968).

The most recent general study of political institutions is a multi-volume work, *Histoire des institutions françaises au moyen âge*, edited by F. Lot and R. Fawtier, 3 vols. to date (Paris, 1958-1963). The first of these volumes is a useful survey of the institutions of the main territorial principalities. The second volume, on royal institutions, is disappointing in many respects. Students therefore will still find useful the older works of A. Luchaire: *Histoire des institutions monarchiques de la France sous les premiers capétiens,* 2 vols. (Paris, 1891), and *Manuel des institutions françaises: Periode des capétiens directs* (Paris, 1902). Also useful are surveys by the French legal historians: J. Declareuil, *Histoire générale du droit français des origines à 1789* (Paris, 1925); A. Esmein, *Cours élémentaire d'histoire du droit français* (Paris, 1903); and F. Olivier-Martin *Histoire du droit français des origines à la révolution* (Paris, 1948).

A number of books and articles deal with the French realm as a concept or with aspects of French kingship. Among these are C. Wood, "Regnum Francie: A Problem in Capetian Administrative Usage," *Traditio* XXIII (1967), 117-147; J. Strayer, "France: The Holy Land, the Chosen People, and the Most Christian King," in *Action and Conviction in Early Modern Europe*, edited by T. Rabb and J. Siegel (Princeton, 1969), pp. 3-16; B. Guenée, "Etat et nation en France au Moyen Âge," *Revue Historique* 237 (1967), 17-30; and P. Schramm, *Der König von Frankreich,* 2 vols. (Weimar, 1939). Books that touch on French kingship but deal with broader European phenomena are M. Bloch, *Les rois thaumaturges* (Paris, 1924), and E. Kantorowicz, *The King's Two Bodies* (Princeton, 1957). Finally, one might mention an older work by A. Brachet, *Pathologie mentale des rois de France* (Paris, 1903). This last book is not a trustworthy source, but it is often cited because of its interesting speculations.

Monographs devoted to the lives and reigns of specific kings form an important part of the historical literature of medieval France. Of rather variable value, these may be listed in order of reigns as follows: F. Lot and L. Halphen, *Le régne de Charles le Chauve, 842-877* (Paris, 1902); E. Favre, *Eudes, comte de Paris et roi de France 882-898* (Paris, 1892); P. Lauer, *Robert I et Raoul de Bourgogne, rois de France* (Paris, 1912); P. Lauer, *Louis IV d'Outremer* (Paris, 1900); F. Lot, *Les deniers Carolingiens: Lothaire, Louis V, Charles de Lorraine* (Paris, 1892); F. Lot, *Études sur le régne de Hugues Capet* (Paris, 1903); C. Pfister, *Études sur le régne de Robert le Pieux* (Paris, 1885); A. Fliche, *Le régne de Philippe Ier, roi de France* (Paris, 1912); A. Luchaire, *Louis VI le Gros, Annales de sa vie et de son régne* (Paris, 1890); M. Pacaut, *Louis VII et son royaume* (Paris, 1964); A. Cartellieri, *Philipp II August, König von Frankreich,* 5 vols. (Leipzig, 1899-1922); C. Petit-

Dutailis, *Étude sur la vie et la régne de Louis VIII* (Paris, 1894); M. Labarge, *Saint Louis: The Life of Louis IX of France* (Toronto, 1968); C. V. Langlois, *Le régne de Philippe III le Hardi* (Paris, 1887); P. Lehugeur, *Histoire de Philippe le Long, roi de France (1316-1322)*, 2 vols. (Paris, 1897-1931); R. Cazelles,*La société politique et la crise de la royauté sous Philippe de Valois* (Paris, 1958); C. Delachenal, *Histoire de Charles V*, 5 vols. (Paris, 1909-1931); P. Kendall, *Louis XI: "the Universal Spider"* (New York, 1970).

The best of those works are the ones dealing with the reigns of Philip I through Louis VII. No adequate study exists for the important reign of Philip IV, while the reigns of his three sons are in serious need of restudy. For Philip VI, Cazelles' recent work is only a partial treatment. Much of the basic research on this reign was done by Jules Viard, who never wrote a comprehensive synthesis but whose many articles are listed in Cazelles' bibliography. The important reign of John II is largely dealt with by Delachenal, whose exhaustively factual study of the life and reign of Charles V neglects important questions of social and economic history but has the merit of having used manuscript sources outside Paris. The reign of Charles VII is in need of restudy, while that of Louis XI lacks an adequate synthesis. Kendall bases his study of Louis XI mainly on the dispatches of the Milanese ambassadors, of which he is co-editor. The detailed workings of the government under Louis XI still await an ambitious historian. Much can be learned about this reign and about fifteenth-century France generally by reading P. S. Lewis, *Later Medieval France: The Polity* (London, 1968), an excerpt of which is included in this volume. The organization of Lewis' book, however, makes some of his material difficult to use.

Related to the histories of individual kings and reigns are books devoted to important royal princes. For princely *apanages* the essential introduction is C. Wood, *The French Apanages and the Capetian Monarchy, 1224-1328* (Cambridge, Mass., 1966). On individual apanaged princes, see E. Boutaric, *Saint Louis et Alphonse de Poitiers* (Paris, 1870); J. Petit, *Charles de Valois (1270-1325)* (Paris, 1900); J. M. Richard, *Une petite-niéce de Saint Louis, Mahaut, comtesse d'Artois et de Bourgogne (1302-1329)* (Paris, 1887); D. Secousse, *Memoires pour servir à l'histoire de Charles II, roi de Navarre et comte d'Evreux, surnommé le Mauvais* (Paris, 1758); F. Lehous, *Jean de France, duc de Berri: sa vie, son action politique (1340-1416)*, 3 vols. (Paris, 1966-1968); R. Vaughan, *Philip the Bold* (Cambridge, Mass., 1962); R. Vaughan, *John the Fearless: The Growth of Burgundian Power* (London, 1966); and H. Stein, *Charles de France, frére de Louis XI* (Paris, 1921). For the period of bitter rivalry among the princes at the end of the fourteenth century, see the following: J. d'Avout, *La querelle des Armagnacs et des Bourguignons* (Paris, 1943); M. Nordberg, *Les Ducs et la royauté' Études sur la rivalité des ducs d'Orléans et de Bourgogne, 1392-1407* (Uppsala, 1964); and M. Rey, *Les finances royales sous Charles VI: Les causes du déficit* (Paris, 1965).

There also are important works on periods of French monarchical history. The classic study of the Carolingians and their decline is L. Halphen, *Charlemagne et l'Empire carolingien* (Paris, 1949). The best works on the breakdown of royal power in the ninth and tenth centureis are those of which excerpts are reprinted in this book: J. Dhondt, *Études sur la naissance des principautés territoriales en France* (Bruges, 1948), and A. Lewis, *The Development of Southern French and Catalan Society, 718-1050* (Austin, 1965).

The entire period from the late ninth century until the reign of Louis VII is surveyed from the point of view of the main political events in another work from which this volume contains an excerpt: J. Calmette, *Le Réveil Capetien* (Paris, 1948), a book which suffers somewhat from its nationalistic bias. For the workings of the royal government in a period of limited documentation, a superb study, based on a detailed analysis of the extent royal charters, is J. F. Lemarignier, *Le gouvernement royal aux premiers temps capétiens (987-1108)* (Paris, 1965), parts of which are also reprinted here. An important earlier work uses many of the same documents for a somewhat different purpose: W. Newman, *Le domaine royal sous les premiers capétiens* (Paris, 1937). Two excellent books in English translation which touch upon the French monarchy during the rule of the direct Capetians are R. Fawtier, *The Capetian Kings of France* (London and New York, 1960), and C. Petit-Dutaillis, *The Feudal Monarchy in France and England* (London, 1936), now in paperback as a Harper Torchbook). Another French work in English translation is the best one-volume narrative account of the early Valois period, E. Perroy, *The Hundred Years War* (London, 1951, now in paperback as a Capricorn book).

One can only summarize a few of the many books available on the institutions of the French monarchy. On the chancery, see O. Morel, *Le grande chancellerie royale et l'expedition des lettres royaux de l'avènement de Philippe de Valois à la fin du XIVe siècle (1328-1400)* (Paris, 1900), and G. Tessier, *Diplomatique royal francaise* (Paris, 1962). There is no monographic study devoted strictly to the Parlement of Paris in the middle ages, but the student is directed to the following works: F. Aubert, *Histoire du Parlement de Paris*, vol. 1 (Paris, 1894); E. Maugis, *Histoire du Parlement de Paris de l'avènement des rois Valois à la mort d'Henri IV*, 3 vols. (Paris, 1913-1916); and J. Shennan, *The Parlement of Paris* (London, 1968). On an important application of law in the late middle ages, see M. Keen, *The Laws of War in the Later Middle Ages* (London and Toronto, 1965). On the recently studied legal profession, see F. Pegues, *The Lawyers of the Last Capetians* (Princeton, 1962), partly reprinted in this volume; also B. Guenée, *Tribunaux et gens de justice dans le bailliage de Senlis à la fin du moyen âge* (Paris, 1963), and J. Strayer, *Les gens de justice du Languedoc sous Philippe le Bel* (Toulouse, 1970).

For the personnel of French local administration, the basic reference work, although not perfectly accurate, is G. Dupont-Ferrier, *Gallia Regia, ou État des officiers royaux de bailliages et des sénéchausées de 1328 à 1515*, 6 vols. (Paris, 1942). For the institutions of two important regions, see P. Dognon, *Les institutions politiques et administratives du pays de Languedoc, du XIIIe siècle aux guerres de religion* (Toulouse, 1895), and J. Strayer, The Administration of Normandy *under St. Louis* (Cambridge, Mass., 1932). Space does not permit mention of several excellent works on the administration of specific districts, but see the two articles that are partially reprinted here: J. Fesler, "French Field Administration: The Beginnings," *Comparative Studies in Society and History,* V (1962), 76-111; and J. Rogozinski, "The Counsellors of the Seneschal of Beaucaire and Nîmes, 1250-1350," *Speculum* XLIV (1969), 421-438. See also J. Strayer, "Viscounts and Viguiers under Philip the Fair," *Speculum* XXXVIII (1963), 145-255, and J. Henneman, *"Enquéteurs-Réformateurs* and Fiscal Officers in Fourteenth Century France," *Traditio* XXIV (1968), 309-349.

On royal finance, a still useful oder work is A. Vuitry, *Études sure le régime financier de la France avant la Revolution de 1789,* 2 vols. (Paris, 1878-1883). On the period after 1285, the three principal works are J. Strayer and C. Taylor, *Studies in Early French Taxation* (Cambridge, Mass., 1939); J. Henneman, *Royal Taxation in Fourteenth-Century France: The Development of War Financing, 1322-1356* (Princeton, 1971); and M. Rey, *Le domaine du roi et les finances extraordinaires sous Charles VI, 1388-1413* (Paris, 1965).

On central representative assemblies, the badly outdated classic work is G. Picot, *Histoire des états généraux, considerés au point de vue de leur influence sur le gouvernement de la France de 1355 à 1614,* 4 vols. 2nd ed. (Paris, 1888). Recent research has not yet produced a major synthesis, but the following studies should be pointed out: G. Langmuir, "Politics and Parliaments in the early Thirteenth Century," *Studies Presented to the International Commission for the History of Representative and Parliamentary Institutions* XXIX (1966), 47-62; C. Taylor, "The Composition of Baronial Assemblies in France, 1315-1320," *Speculum,* XXIX (1954), 433-459; C. Taylor, "French Assemblies and Subsidy in 1321," *Speculum* XLIII (1968), 217-244; J. Henneman, "The French Estates General and Reference Back to Local Constituents, 1343-1355," *Studies Presented to the International Commission for the History of Representative and Parliamentary Institutions,* XXXIX (1970), 29-52; P. S. Lewis, "The Failure of the French Medieval Estates," *Past and Present* XXIII (1962), 3-24; and J. R. Major, *Representative Institutions in Renaissance France, 1421-1559* (Madison, 1960).

There are many good studies of provincial Estates and regional representative insitutions. Three particularly useful ones are A. Coville, *Les états de Normandie, leurs origines et leur développement au XIVe siècle* (Paris, 1894); T. Bisson, *Assemblies and Representation in Languedoc in the Thirteenth Century* (Princeton, 1964); and A. Thomas, *Les états provinciaux de la France centrale sous Charles VII* 2 vols. (Paris, 1879). Assemblies of Estates, both central and regional, remain subjects of considerable scholarly debate, as do many other aspects of the medieval French monarchy.